PASSING THE BATON TO MY FAMILY

Passing the Baton to My Family

Ken Babington

My Legacy 2100

My Legacy 2100

Copyright © 2023 by Ken Babington

    All rights internationally reserved. No part of this publication may be reproduced, stored in a retrieval system, or transmitted in any form or by any means, electronic, mechanical, photocopying, recording, or otherwise, without written permission of the publisher, except by a reviewer who may quote brief passages embodied in a review with appropriate credits. Trademarked names may appear throughout the book. Rather than use a trademark symbol with every occurrence of a trademarked name, names are used in an editorial fashion with no intention of infringement of the respective owner's trademark. The information in this book is distributed on an "as is" basis, without warranty. Although every precaution has been taken in the preparation of this work, neither the author nor the publisher shall have any liability to any person or entity with respect to any loss, damage, or mental or emotional impact caused or alleged to be caused directly or indirectly by the information contained in this book.

Printed in the United States of America

Photos and Illustrations licensed from Shutterstock.com
or are in the public domain unless otherwise attributed.

    Babington, Ken
        Passing the Baton to My Family / by Ken Babington.
            p. cm.

Also by Ken Babington

Not My God –
My Life As The Pastor Of The Man
Who Murdered John Lennon

To all those
who embrace the
spiritual baton from us

> "One generation shall praise Thy works to another, and shall declare Thy mighty acts."
>
> — Psalm 145.4

FOREWORD

Between these covers, I have put together a variety of "words of wisdom" as well as my own background. I love you, and at my age, this is me passing the baton of life to you. True, I am not gone YET, but I am closer than ever before.

Please read this as from your Paw Paw who loves you. You have known me all your life. I really strive to be nice, fun, non-offensive, and encouraging. True, I am strongly opinionated (but teachable with truth and facts); I am an unashamed conservative Christian, with no apology. The Bible is 100% accurate. Jesus is the only way to God for eternal life. You are both responsible and accountable for the way you live. You were created by God, and at Creation,

God designed America, knowing where the nation would be on this day.

America is in your hands, and this book is written to help you find His purpose for your life.

I love you,

Paw Paw

MY FAMILY

Cheryl (Maw Maw) and I met in December, 1964, and were married on February 22, 1969. We had been married 43 years when she died suddenly on October 24, 2012. Cheryl was a Director in Mary Kay Cosmetics, but in 1984, she decided to be a "stay-at-home" Mom. For the next 28 years, she home-schooled our children and grandchildren, and she helped other families do the same. Her ministry, passion, and life, were children and the next generation to come. She loved her children and grandchildren with an unbelievable passion. After her death, I knew instantly: I cannot take her place. I decided to write our 13 grandchildren. That weekly ministry began in 2013, and has not stopped, nor will it.

In October, 2013, I met Sylvia, and we were married on March 28, 2015. Sylvia has four children, 10 grandchildren, and one great-grandchild, David, who was born on April 26, 2023 (congratulations Josh and Megan!) At some point (I think it was 2016), I decided to include Sylvia's grandchildren in the weekly mailing, and each of her 10 grandchildren and David receive a weekly letter from me, with Bible study material enclosed. The children and grandchildren from Cheryl make up my biological family. The children and grandchildren from Sylvia make up my blended family. Sylvia and her husband owned an electrical contracting company. The Lord called her into ministry, and her family joined her on the road. For 10 years, her four children went to virtually every state in the U.S.A. Sylvia was in music evangelism, and her ministry was nationwide. Her entire family lived and traveled in a 5th wheel dually pickup truck, carrying a 45 foot trailer to live in, and Sylvia did the driving. Sylvia, her husband, and all four children, were in the truck, and America was their mission field.

Today, Sylvia has an amazingly interesting ministry. Each day, she sends out a few Bible verses to approximately 75 individuals, one-by-one. She has been in ministry all her adult life, and that ministry continues today.

SPOILER ALERT

This book is written specifically to three generations: my children, my grandchildren, and my great grandchildren. It is also written to my four children "blended in by marriage", my 10 blended grandchildren, and four blended great-grandchildren. In addition to these people; the church family at First Baptist Cocoa Beach, friends, and finally to the public. I do have an abundance of children in my spiritual discipleship. There is the proverbial "elephant in the room" that must be addressed, with a spoiler alert.

This book is written to give children life principles from me, others, senior citizens, and from the Bible. True, children can absorb and apply material. HOWEVER, the Biblical model is that children learn these principles from their parents. I now present to you two "spoiler alerts". Sorry, it is too late to close the book, or ignore the following.

To Mom and Dad: YOU ARE RESPONSIBLE to teach these (and other) principles to your children as they grow up. You cannot "delegate" that responsibility to anyone!! YOU are the one responsible, and at some point in the future, you will give an account to the Lord Jesus for the faithful stewardship of your parental responsibility (1 Corinthians 4:2).

Children, at some point in the future, you will most likely be an adult, get married, and have children. At that moment, your name is spiritually put into the comments for #1 above: YOU ARE RESPONSIBLE. In reality, you are responsible now to submit to your parents as they train you to be a parent.

As I write this, my youngest blood-relative, Henry, has a couple months to go before his birth. For Henry, and all who read this book; when you are age 76, it is my heart's desire you will be instilling these principles into the lives of those in your legacy. May you live out Joshua 24:15 and Psalm 145:4.

Aside: Henry Elliott Griffin was born at 10:32 A.M. on Wednesday, November 30, 2022. He weighed in at five pounds 13 ounces, and 19 inches tall!! Welcome to the family, Henry. Someday, YOU will be a Paw Paw.

One more thought: Generic use of "son" must include son-daughter!

I love you,
Paw Paw
Proverbs 17:6; Proverbs 23:26

DISCLAIMER

There is a "movement" in America that I must address up-front, for your benefit. With me being in elementary school in the 1950's, high-school in the 1960's, and a married, Dad, with a job, by 1970, I have seen the effects of this movement. Here I am at the very opening comments on the book to encourage you, and I am being ruthlessly blunt, with no apology.

This "movement" started around 1820 when people began to dismantle the nation that was birthed a few decades earlier. By 2022, the "movement" has all but taken over America, and it will be your generation that will either pay the price, or reign in the destruction.

It is rare to find an honest politician who is not under the thumb of THE PARTY or lobbyists. It is rare to find a true journalist who will simply report news without commentary or opinion. In 2022 America, the First Amendment is kept in an antique store, and factual history has been vetoed by people with an agenda to destroy America. It is a battle for the heart of America, and if you sit on the sidelines, your grandchildren will grow up in a totally different America than we have even today.

In 2022 America, the nation is going WOKE. The church is going WOKE. Good is considered evil, and evil is presented as good. The history of America is being ignored as we hear lies about our weak foundation. The financial outlook for America is bleak, yet those elected are addicted to spending your finances. We have laws for immigration, yet millions cross our borders illegally, with impunity, and with our financial support. My concern is almost endless, but for this disclaimer, I will only use one illustration.

Conservative Christians nationwide are being portrayed as domestic terrorists because we love America, and say with confident accuracy that our country was founded on Biblical principles. That is a true statement, and I will BRIEFLY explain that. In 1620, the Mayflower Compact honors Jesus. in 1639, the Constitution of Connecticut honored Jesus. In 1647, public schools were started because of "The Olde deluder satan Law". In 1647, public schools were started so children could learn how to read the Bible. The McGuffey reader sold over 100 million books for public schools. Children learned to read, using Bible verses in the McGuffy Reader. In 1811, People vs. Ruggles, Ruggles was found guilty; he was given three months in jail, and fined $500 for blaspheming Jesus in Kingsbury, New York. Harvard, Princeton, and Yale were started to train pastors. The Declaration of Independence talks of our Creator and His providential oversight of our nation. On top of the Washington Monument is "God be praised". The frontal bust of Moses is at ceiling level, directly in front of the Speaker of the House podium in Congress. In 1892, the UNANIMOUS decision of the United States Supreme Court in the case United States v. Church of the Holy Trinity (143 US.457-1892), the Court unanimously decided, in writing, that America is a Christian nation. This list is almost endless, but one more illustration. In the first Congress, after the Revolution, the very first Speaker of the House was a pastor from New York. Do your research on the above, and find more historical facts. America was founded on Christian principles, and the Supreme Court unanimously labeled our country a Christian nation.

It is your turn to lead America. This book is written to help you do that. You will read about manners, rules for civility, family principles from Proverbs, character, and more. At age 76, my days on earth are numbered, and I want to pass the spiritual baton of life to you before I am gone. You decide how you will live, and I encourage you to love Jesus, love your family, love America, and live out your life with eternal purpose IN JESUS.

I love you,
Paw Paw

INTRODUCTION

This book is written for my biological and blended family; and if that is not you, please keep reading. My three children have a total of 13 children, and five biological grandchildren (my five biological great-grandchildren). Good news: I have more children, grandchildren, and great-grandchildren through my blended family. Great news. I have more children, grandchildren, and great grandchildren, in my spiritual legacy. So, after all of the above, to whom is this book written? TO YOU.

Truth time. I plan to give this book to some of the above, and thankfully you may have purchased the book you are now holding. More truth. This one book could prove to be the best financial investment of your life. Try this: my goal and objective in this book is to equip you, and prepare you to live out Ephesians 2:8-10. Yes, there is more. By you living out Ephesians 2:8-10, you and your family (biological, blended, and spiritual) could very well change your community, state, America, and the world itself before the 22nd century begins. That, beloved, is a worthy plan, objective, and life goal.

WHY IS THIS BOOK WRITTEN?!

With so many books on families, why write another one? Who even cares? Of what redeeming value could this book be? The answer is brief, with meat on the bone: America; the Church; your family; YOU are the "WHY".

I was born in the summer of 1946. My Dad was born in March, 1919, and Mom was born in February, 1922. I never met my Mom's dad. He died in 1928 when she was six years old. My Grandmother on Mom's side was born around 1890, and I have memories of her being friendly, usually helpful, and nice. She died around 1970. My Dad's Dad (Pappy) was born in 1889, and his wife (Gramma) was born in 1890. Pappy died at age 94 in 1984 (I was 37). Gramma was 99 when she died in 1989. The dates were intentional. Gramma and Pappy were married 71 years, and Mom and Dad were a few days away from their 65th anniversary when Dad died.

Life was so much different prior to 1900. While it may not be factual, a quote is attributed to Charles H. Duell, the Commissioner of the U.S. Patents Office, in 1899. He was quoted as saying, "Everything that can be invented has already been invented". I guess he was wrong. When my grandparents were children, bicycles were not commonly produced for children. That did not happen until they were well over 40 years old. It was after my Dad was born (1919) when about one in four homes had a telephone, nationwide. When my grandparents were children, they used the "out house", outside their home for bodily waste. When they were children, a refrigerator was almost unheard of. Henry Ford made his Model-T Ford around 1908, and his assembly line started around 1913. Life was so much different for my grandparents than it is for my grandchildren. It was around 1960 when over 50% of the homes in America had a television. Ours was a 13" screen, black and white shows, no color! Before 6:00 A.M., there was a test pattern only, for a screen. At 11:00 P.M., they displayed the American flag, and played the National Anthem before putting the test pattern on the screen until 6:00 A.M. Oh has America changed. Check me out on this. The third time Elvis Presley sang on the Ed Sullivan show (January 6, 1957), they only filmed him from the waist up. Life has changed since then.

AMERICA BY GENERATIONS

There is a very specific reason for **THIS** book, at **THIS** time. I am the last major generational shift. Born in 1946, I was an early "Baby Boomer". Today, 2022, I am considered an antique, relic, has-been. On Monday, August 16, 2022, a friend my age told me, "When our generation is gone, America will be gone". Regardless of your opinion, that was a startling comment. On the next day, August 17, 2022, a Navy buddy of mine from 1966-1969, on the USS Atule (SS-403), (Lester Benoit), sent me four pictures with captions.

1. Washington in his boat with his troops – "hard times create strong men"
2. The men who signed the Declaration of Independence – "strong men create good times"
3. Four teenage guys with college sweatshirts, and their fists held to the sky – "good times create weak men"
4. Anarchy: fires in the streets – "weak men produce hard times"

Again, regardless of your age or opinion, those are four startling analogies.

I began thinking of those two events in my life, within a 24 hour period, and very quickly came up with an analogy.

1. The Great Depression produced the World War II soldier
2. The World War II soldier produced the Baby Boomers
3. The Baby Boomers produced the Millennials
4. The Millennials produced 2022 America with a possible depression on the horizon

Once more, regardless of your age or opinion, that is a startling analogy.

Again, as a result of those two things on August 16, 2022, I began research on generations, and easily found these pieces to a multi-generational American puzzle. Dates may vary a little, depending on your source.

1. The Lost Generation: Born between 1883-1900

- Disoriented
- Wandering
- Directionless
- Industrial Revolution
- Strict conservative values

2. The Greatest Generation: Born between 1900-1927
    - Spanish Flu 1918-1920
    - Rapid technology: radio, telephone, automobile
    - Income inequality
    - Golden Age of Hollywood
    - "Swing Generation" in music and dancing
    - Alive when the Great Depression hit America in 1929
    - Kept going in difficult times
    - Knew how to withstand hardships
    - Fought in World War II

3. The Silent Generation: Born between 1928-1945
    - Children of the Great Depression
    - Followed the rules
    - Not risk takers
    - Frugal, with good work ethics
    - Korean War Veterans
    - Civil Rights advocates
    - Rock-n-Roll music
    - Fewer people in this generation

4. Baby Boomer Generation: Born between 1945-1965
    - Students during education reform
    - Ideological confrontation
    - Counter-culture: Hippies; Woodstock; crime; drugs
    - Political instability: 1968 Democrat National Convention – riots and fires

- Increased affluence
- Increased government subsidies
- Drug epidemic on the streets across America
- Draft dodgers left the country
- Vietnam conflict was a political football, with America as the loser
- Vietnam era veterans were not received well at home (I was in the Navy then)
- Revolution in music

5. Generation X: Born between 1965-1980
    - Latch-key Generation – empty home after school
    - Reduced parental supervision
    - More divorces – mother working – child care facilities
    - MTV and video games
    - Disaffected by society
    - Cynical
    - Slackers

6. Generation Y (Millennial Generation): Born between 1981-1996
    - The first global generation
    - Less religious
    - Children of Baby Boomers and early Generation X parents
    - Parents of Alpha Generation
    - Early days of the Internet
    - They tend to have fewer children

7. Generation Z: Born 1997-2009
    - Known as "Zoomers"; "Post-millenials"
    - Grew up with iPhone
    - Numerous social changes in America
    - Legalization of same sex marriage

- Possible foreign born parents
- Shifting gender identifications
- Many are raised in cities, rather than rural
- Delay marriage
- Grew up with technological inventions
- Use a lot of anonymous social medias

8. Generation Alpha: Born between 2010-2025
   - First completely 21st Century Generation
   - Raised on internet, social media, mobile devices
   - Fully digital technology
   - Streaming, less television, and more social networking online
   - Sexting
   - Falling birth rate
   - Issues with allergies, obesity, health, due to technology
   - Fewer personal friendships

{**DISCLAIMER:** The above dates may differ a little, based on what "chart" you may use.}

As I said above, I am the last major generation shift. The Lost Generation is gone. The Greatest Generation is dying off rapidly. The Silent Generation is dwindling quickly. All three of those generations are virtually gone, or in nursing homes with dementia or Alzheimer's. Any "words of wisdom" from those three generations must, by default, be in print already. However, the new, current, "Senior Generation" is the Baby Boomers (1945-1965), and with me being born in 1946, I am on the older side of that "Senior Generation". I am 76 years old, living on borrowed time. The estimated life expectancy of a male is 78 years old (between 74-80 on various charts).

THEREFORE, if I want to say anything to my family, I better get it written before breakfast. ASIDE: I am writing this early Thursday morning, August 18, 2022. Last night at 9:42 P.M., I got a text from my 12 year old grand-daughter, Rose (I lovingly call her Rosalini). Her text read: "Do you have things you want me to pray for in the next week". I discreetly told her about the book and the time-crunch I am on. I want this book finished, edited, printed, and presented to my immediate family BEFORE CHRISTMAS, and I am just starting to write it in mid-August, 2022. Rose has no idea she is praying about her own Christmas gift. ASIDE over.

As a young boy in Jacksonville, our next-door neighbors were two sisters, born around 1870 (Ms. Russell and Ms. North). My grandparents were all born between 1885-1891, and I knew Dad's parents until I was around 40. Years ago, funeral homes began calling me to do funerals for many people born before 1900. As a Pastor (started in 1977), I have done funeral services for church members who were born before 1900. On the opposite end, I have great-grandchildren in the Generation Alpha (2010-2025), and without exception, ALL of my great-grandchildren are Generation Alpha. Again, I am the older end of the current transitional generation, and I MUST GIVE YOU COUNSEL; and that counsel must be in writing.

I heard my grandparents talk about their childhood. Another ASIDE: I did a funeral in Melbourne, Florida a few years ago. After the service, a man asked me if I had any relatives in Atlanta. I said yes, my grandparents lived there. He said, "he may have been my Boy Scout Leader". My immediate response was: "then I have seen your footprint on the ceiling of his basement at 968 Williams Mill Road". We both laughed, and he shared several fascinating stories about my Pappy. For me, it was my Pappy who encouraged me to quit chewing my fingernails. I stopped that habit at about age 10. It was my Pappy who taught me fool-proof correct grammar for "I" and/or "me" in a sentence: The bus stopped for you and ME. You and I got on the bus. The key is simple. Take the other person out of the sentence, and which is correct: I or me? 100% accurate. Pappy would NEVER eat at a restaurant with a sign that says "Good Eats". He said "If they have poor grammar, then they are probably poor cooks".

Time for another ASIDE. Back in the 1950's, it was a RARE treat to go to a restaurant! In December, 1958, Gramma and Pappy took my brother, Tom, and me (grammatically correct) to Mexico, by car, for two weeks. In Mexico City, Gramma took us to a bullfight because Pappy did not like to watch a bullfight. I have so many memories and life lessons, and I must put them in print for you!! Two more. I have only one handwritten letter from Pappy, and a copy of that letter is in this book. Also, LONG before personal computers, Pappy spent 30 years doing research, and around 1965, he did a hand-written family genealogy, back to around 1635!! I still have that, and his chart has been updated twice by me. His chart is almost three feet by 4 feet in size, handwritten.

I am the older end of the current transitional generation. I was taught life principles by visible example from people born between 1870-1890, and later this year, my great-grandson, Henry, will be born. As I edit today, December 8, 2022, Henry is a week old.

This book is dedicated to those before me, so those after me have a standard for life.

MY CHILDHOOD - YOUNG ADULT

Born in 1946, and being a Baby Boomer, life for me as a child was fun. Dad worked for Southern Bell, and until I was four years old, Mom was a book-keeper in a bank. Back then, there were few daycare centers, and Lannie Mae took care of Tom and me. I have memories of us driving her home, and she was amazing. Walter was our mail man, and he was always ready to play football or baseball with us. I remember we had milk delivered, but I have no solid memory of who delivered it. I remember the night before my first day at school. Tom and I were going to walk to school, and I remember asking him if we would need to stop and take a break. I remember my brother saying "No. I think we can make it". School was about half a mile away. Of course, we made it.

Mom and Dad. Dad was a Navy World War II Veteran. He was stationed on the USS Savannah (CL-42). His ship was bombed on September 11, 1943, and over 200 of the 600 man crew died that day. You can find that online. I remember Dad on his Cushman scooter, giving Tom and me a ride together. One weekend, Dad went duck hunting, and came back empty-handed. Dad built an entire garage by himself. One day, he came home from work with an alligator about two feet long. We kept it in a metal container for about a week before Mom said it had to go. Same premise with a black snake. Dad brought a black snake home from my baseball practice. Mom said, "Either the snake leaves, or I leave". I never saw the snake again.

Dad worked for Southern Bell for 43 years. He both crossed the union picket line in management, after honoring the picket line as a cable splicer. Even today, if I see a telephone employee with scissors on his belt, I say "nice looking snips"; and he knows! One time, Dad took me down a man-hole with him on 5th Avenue in Indialantic, south side of the street, by the river. It was great. One day Dad went deep-sea fishing, and came home seasick. He called in to work, and took a vacation day. He worked 43 years, and never once called in sick. His work ethics were strong, and Dad was very loyal to those who worked with him.

Mom worked in the bank, but became a stay-at-home Mom by 1950. We had breakfast, lunch (maybe), and supper as a family. Dad said the blessing at every meal. Mom was a great cook, and her fried chicken would make

Colonel Sanders a General. Mom always made mayonnaise because Dad loved it. Mom and Dad had an idea, and I cannot remember who said what. Mom would wet Dad's shirts in liquid starch, roll them up, and put them in the refrigerator overnight. Probably Mom said, "somebody should put this starch in a bottle and so we can just spray it on". Dad said, "that will never work". Between Mom and Dad, they taught all four boys to cook, iron, wash and fold clothes, vacuum, clean house, and more. They laughingly said we would make good wives.

MORE MEMORIES

Mom had four sisters and a brother, and we were always together as a big family. Mom's sister, Ruth, was married to Ovid Gano, and they bought a lot on Big Swan Lake in Melrose, Florida. During the summer, for several years, we drove the 90 minute trip every Friday afternoon. The boys swam and played while the adults worked. We did our share of manual labor, but the weekends were cousins, aunts, uncles, swimming, and lots of food.

One summer, when I was about age 10, I went to a Bible Camp. I have no memory of a decision, or any specific teaching, but I do remember the facilities were old, even for 1956. The only spiritual memory I have is one afternoon when Tom and I were on the back porch, and Mom was talking to us about John 14. All those years, with every Sunday, and one memory.

Okay, two memories. In our Methodist Church one Sunday, I did the Catholic Cross. Mom saw me do it, and oh my, did I have some quick explaining to do.

After high school, I attended the University of Florida in August, 1964. I pledged the same fraternity as my brother, Tom, and roomed in the dormitory with a friend from high school. After my first semester, I was home for Christmas, and went to a dance. While there, it turned out my friend, Alex Samsel, was also a friend of Cheryl Shook, and Alex introduced us that night. Cheryl and I were married in 1969. Our first child was born in 1970, and that same Alex Samsel was the one person I called to join me in the delivery waiting room until Lisa was born. Alex and I remained close friends for almost 60 years, and I was his pastor for over 20 years, until his death this year, 2022.

Cheryl and I were married for 43 years, until her sudden death on Wednesday, October 24, 2012. I remember a phrase I have used countless times, and will continue using it. "She was married to me, but she lived for her children and grandchildren". Our three children, and our 13 grandchildren were her life passion. She loved each one of them, and displayed that love individually, in too many ways to record. They really were her life's passion. Sweet Winnie was an infant when Cheryl held her, just weeks before her death. Once more: she was married to me, but truly lived for her children and grandchildren. My counsel for all generations of our family is this: learn about Maw Maw from Lisa, Judy Kay, Ron, Blake, Shelby, Ashleigh, Travis, Sam, Caroline, Afton, and Ben. The younger ones may have memories, but the older ones will be eager to tell you a Maw Maw story. Keep her memories going to future generations.

The couple's conference was Friday – Sunday, March 5-7, 1976. I left home spiritually dead without even knowing that. When I arrived home less than 48 hours later, I was born again, living for eternity. The weekend theme was: "YOU ARE ACCOUNTABLE". At some point on Saturday, the key speaker, Kay Arthur, was teaching a class to the 200 people (100 married couples). I was seated, with no invitation, no music, and no emotion, talking to God Himself. No one heard me, and no one noticed any commotion from me. The conversation went this way, and I quote: "God, if You are real; and Jesus, if You died for me; and if I am really accountable to You, then YOU change, because I have no desire to change". Discussion finished. I kept listening to the lesson, and no one would have guessed the Lord had already responded to me. Without me knowing it at that moment, the new birth had taken place, and the changes had begun. Completely out of character, I paid $20.00 for the cassette tapes (ask an old person about cassette tapes) for the weekend. On our way home Sunday afternoon, with five other people in the car, I remember saying, "I want to spend the rest of my life telling people the Lord can change their life like He has changed my life. But I couldn't talk for 30 minutes". Today, people laugh when I tell that story.

It was Saturday, March 6, 1976, when I had the conversation with the Lord. That was four months before my 30th birthday. I was back in my home by 2:00 P.M. the next day (Sunday). By Monday evening, March 8, 1976, I owned three brand new books, and as I write this book in September, 2022, all three of those books are on my desk at home. That Monday, I bought a NASB Bible, Vine's Expository Dictionary, and a Strong's Exhaustive Concordance. Friday morning, March 5, 1976, I had never heard of any of those three books. Today, 46 years later, I am still using those three books literally every day.

Within three years (1979) I was teaching other men how to study the Bible, and I had written a 52-week discipleship system that I still use in 2022, with a few changes. By 1979, I had memorized well over 100 verses, and my passion deepened on a daily basis. But those three years were not without ISSUES.

From August 1, 1977, our home was open to anyone, anytime, and YES, they did show up. Our pastor was an evangelist, and I think we baptized almost 100 people per year. My passion was to disciple these new converts, and I loved it. I thought it was a perfect fit: an evangelistic pastor, and a discipler as the associate. Within a few months, a church in our community needed a pastor, and a friend of that church, put us together. Without my knowledge, my pastor was becoming threatened by our church befriending me. He told the other church lies about me, and in April 1978, he brought me into his office to fire me. At the deacon meeting later that week, he told the deacons I was leaving. One deacon asked me if I thought my ministry there was over, I said "No sir". He then asked why I was leaving, and I said, "You will need to ask the pastor". No one asked him, and he said nothing. Months later I did give confidential details to one deacon, and to this day 44 years later, that church still knows no details of exactly why I left.

GRAMMA AND PAPPY

Allow me to introduce you to my Dad's parents. Gramma was born in 1890, and graduated from college to be a teacher. I have no memory of her teaching, but I do remember her. She always answered the telephone with "Alright?!"; ALWAYS. For breakfast, she loved fried bananas. She enjoyed the kitchen, and one solid memory is of Gramma driving the car. I have no memory of Pappy driving. In December 1958, Gramma and Pappy drove Tom and me to Mexico City and Acapulco. We left Melbourne; stopped in Mobile, Alabama; Lake Charles, Louisiana;

McAllen, Texas; and then into Mexico. We saw the cliff divers, and a bullfight. Gramma took us into the bullfight while Pappy stayed outside. He never liked that event. I do remember Gramma voicing her opinions, and my Mom often talked of her and Gramma coming to terms with one another just after Mom and Dad got married in 1942. Aside: Mom and Dad got married six weeks after they met. Mom said she would never encourage anyone to do that. She cautioned: "I did not even know his family". When Gramma was 98, my family (Maw Maw, Lisa, Judy Kay, Ron, and I) asked her numerous questions, with an old-fashion cassette recorder going. We still have that somewhere. Gramma told us about a shooting when she was young, and about a game they played. They sat on the street, and spun-the-bottle. We asked what they did when the bottle stopped spinning. She said, "we spun it again". No confession there.

Pappy worked 47 years for Southern Bell. He would walk a block to a bus stop; ride the bus to downtown Atlanta, and he worked inside the Hurt Building. Pappy spent 30 years doing our family genealogy without a computer. His final genealogy chart was three families: Baber, Babington, Biggerstaff, and our lineage goes back to the early days of the 1600's. In 1635, John Babington was a passenger on THE GLOBE, going to the new world. Pappy hand-wrote the finished chart, and I do have a copy, which I have updated twice. It is ready for the next generation. Pappy loved to read, and he kept a detailed diary of every trip. Gramma and Pappy learned to speak Spanish, and made numerous short-term trips to Mexico. After Pappy retired at age 65, and I remember them going to Mexico for six months. I also have two vivid Pappy-memories. For my 7th birthday (July 19, 1953), Pappy took me to a minor-league baseball game in Atlanta. That was a memorable day. Also, around 1959, Gramma and Pappy were visiting us in Melbourne. We lived on South Babcock Street (244 – now 2320), three blocks south of New Haven Avenue. On the northwest corner of the intersection of Babcock and New Haven, there was a local drug store with a soda fountain. One day, Pappy and I walked up there, and Pappy bought me a soda. I remember sitting next to him in the spinning seat while he watched me spin and drink. I was 13 then. I do have one visible treasure from Pappy, and a picture is in this book. On January 6, 1966, when I was 19, Pappy wrote me a letter. That is the only tangible treasure that I have from him. At some time, I am guessing before that January 6, 1966 letter, I remember being in Gastonia, North Carolina, with Tom, Dad, and Pappy. Pappy took us to his Dad's grave, on the front lawn of the North Carolina Orthopedic Hospital. My great-grandfather helped start the hospital, and he was the first president. Robert Benjamin Babington (1869-1935) was swimming in a creek. His ears got infected, and three days later, at age 66, he died. Pappy spoke with pride as he told us about his Dad. Okay, one more. There is a "family" picture with Mom, Tom, and me. After the picture was taken, we came home, and Mom made us a delicious banana and peanut butter sandwich. Neither Tom nor Mom remembered that, but it is a treasured memory for me every time I see that picture. I suspect I was about age six. At age 10 for me, Gramma and Pappy were about 66-67. I was age 37 when Pappy died (1984), and 42 when Gramma died (1989). At Pappy's funeral (Easter weekend, 1984), Gramma made a memorable comment. She said "I knew this day was coming. I just didn't think it would be this soon". Pappy was 94, and they had been married 71 years. Both of them met all three of my children, and I have a clear mental picture of Pappy, age 91, sitting in a rocking chair holding baby Ron, at less than a year old. Pappy was talking to his great-grandson as if it was a daily routine.

I have so many memories, and I want you to have memories of your Dad, Paw Paw, and Great-Paw Paw. May this book be one of those treasures.

I love you,
Paw Paw

8025 PAUL JONES DRIVE

My childhood (1946-1958) was spent at 8025 Paul Jones Drive in Jacksonville. You should visit our old home. Ask my children!! Dad bought the home for $5,000.00. It was an asbestos shingle-type home, and the front yard was about 50 feet across. There was a crawl space under the house, and we were always playing there. Tom and I played imaginary football (with no actual football) in the front yard. We played baseball in the street (with about 10 boys), and never broke a window! Yes, we did have a real baseball and bat. We played marbles in our dirt driveway, and we spent most of the summer at the park behind our house. Today, going north on I-95 in Jacksonville, at Exit 357 (Edgewood Ave.), you would be about three minutes from my home. If you continue north on I-95, within 15 seconds, you would be at the Trout River Bridge. Between the Trout River Bridge and Exit 357, there is a small neighborhood park on the west side of I-95, and that was "home" for our friends, Tom, and me, all summer. One year, we petitioned the Jacksonville City Commission. They brought in the clay, and we had our own baseball field in the park. Confession time. When my brother, Robert, was born (7-6-1957), Gramma was at our home, taking care of Tom and me. When I heard Robert was born, a friend and I (no memory who!) went to the park that night. We saw adults sitting on the driveway, so we threw rocks at them. We never hit anyone, but they shined lights into the park, as we hid behind a tree (Hey, I was almost 11!). Of course we did not get caught. My days at 8025 were great memories. Without exception, EVERY time I drive by on I-95, I notice that house, and the tree.

    I helped Dad build the garage. We played on the swing in the back yard, and at age eight, I fell while attempting a "trick" on the swing, and broke my left arm. Tom had just done the trick, so I had to try. I remember Mom reading John 14 to Tom and me on the back porch. I remember Dad building the cedar closet next to the front door. One memory I do not have, but Mom told me. Inside the house, on a concrete slab, we had a large furnace. When I was about eight months old, Mom was holding me, and I fell. My head hit the concrete floor. So, I officially have an excuse…One day, my infant brother, Robert, was laying down on his back, and he began throwing up. Someone in the family (not sure who) saw him choking, and rolled him over, saving his life. A few months later, I do remember closing the car door on his hand, and Robert, about one year old, needed three stitches between his thumb and index finger.

    I have so many memories of 8025 Paul Jones Drive. Halloween was almost always fun… almost always. We were usually out for several hours, and came home only to unload our candy. One year, Dad put a ladies stocking over his head to scare us. It worked BIG TIME. One more. I have a picture of Dad and me on the roof of our porch, with the ladder. I had climbed the ladder myself (about age 2 or 3), and Mom and Dad noticed me walking on the roof. So many memories!

I love you,
Paw Paw

THE MOVE TO MELBOURNE

In early 1958, Dad found a 1938, 2-door Plymouth, and bought it for $25.00. He enjoyed working on it, and named the car "HORSE". Tom and I both loved riding in Horse, but never had a desire to help Dad work on it. In the summer of 1958, Dad got transferred to Melbourne. Dad and I took Horse, and Mom, Tom, and Robert drove in our 1953 Mercury. Back then, we only had US-1, and the drive was about four hours. I will NEVER forget the terrible smell of the Indian River as we drove through Titusville.

Our first "home" was the Haven-Aire motel (southeast corner of US-1 and New Haven Avenue in Melbourne). We stayed there six weeks, and almost every day, Mom walked us to a swimming area in the Indian River. While living at the Haven-Aire Motel, the Van Croix theatre was a half-block away. Tom and I could both go, with popcorn and drinks, for $.25 each. Good memories. Within six weeks, Mom and Dad rented a home at 1520 Seminole Ave., just west of Babcock Street, and north of Fee Avenue. Two things happened the exact day we moved there, in July 1958. First, I met the children next door. Today, 64 years later, we are still close, and the dad, Bernie Keene, who was 34 years old then, is now 98 years old. Bernie will be 99 years old on January 20, 2023. Sylvia and I bring him to church with us virtually every Sunday. The second event on day one was selfish. The Little League baseball field was in sight of our house, and I saw two teams in uniform. With permission from Mom, I went to the field, and asked the coach if he needed a player. I was on the Jaycee team all summer. That day, one of the guys I met was Artie Ulmer, and today, we are still friends. Artie went on to be the football coach at Palm Bay High School, and his son is now a local football coach also. That day, I met a young guy who is still a friend, 64 years later. It was awesome, and I must tell one story. When Mom and Dad found a home to rent, our last meal in the motel room was a celebration. We had two rooms with a connecting kitchen. The kitchen area was small, and our card table was good enough to be our dining room table. It made the kitchen crowded, so Dad told Tom and me to pick the table up (with ALL the food on it), and turn the table so we could all fit. We knew to obey Dad, so we went into action. One of us (unsure which – probably ME), lifted the table either higher or lower than the other side. Of course everything fell to the floor. As I remember, Mom and Dad laughed that time.

    One more story. I remember strolling Robert in his stroller on our dirt road. I noticed something by the front left wheel, and Tom took care of that small pygmy rattlesnake.

    From the rental home at 1520 Seminole, Mom and Dad bought the home at 244 South Babcock (later: 2320 South Babcock) in 1959. The 8025 Paul Jones Dr. home cost $5,000. The Babcock home was $18,000, and that was home until 1986. I will share one more TRUE story. Tom Garvin lived about 200 yards south of our home, in Hickory Hills subdivision. I called Tom, knowing he would drive his car

BY OUR HOUSE on the way to school (1964). I asked if he would pick me up, and he said "Yes, for $1.00". I said no thanks, and he honked as he drove past me walking to school. As I remember, gasoline was about $.28 per gallon. Tom is now a multi-millionaire in the Denver area, and yes, we have laughingly remembered that story in the past few years.

Melbourne has been home for me since 1958. In 1966-1969, I was in the Navy. I moved to Atlanta in December 1972, and back to Melbourne in June 1985. I have lived inside Brevard County since then. Again, Melbourne is home for me.

I love you,
Paw Paw

MY TESTIMONY

As a child in Jacksonville (1946-1958), I went to church every Sunday. When we moved to Melbourne, our family joined First Methodist Church, and again, I attended church every Sunday (1958-1964). I was active in the Youth Group, and became our Youth Group (MYF) leader. My senior year in high school, I was the Student Chaplain, and read a daily devotion over the P.A. system to over 2,000 students. Once I graduated from high school, I quit going to church. I believed the Bible was full of errors (so I had been told), and that Jesus was not the only way to Heaven. I even doubted the reality of His death, and I accepted the teaching of Evolution. From high school until Ron McIntosh (1964-1975), I have no memory of anyone talking to me about Jesus. True, in 1969, Cheryl and I got married by a Catholic Priest, but in our pre-marital counseling, his primary concern was that I promised to raise our children in the Catholic Church. I had no desire for any church. So, I easily lied to the Priest, and said YES. From 1964-1975, I do not recall anyone talking to me about Jesus.

In September, 1975 a new employee began working in the same company as Cheryl worked. Her name was Judy McIntosh, and she was excited about the Lord Jesus. Judy and Cheryl talked often, and within a few weeks, Cheryl invited Judy and her husband, Ron, to our house for supper. When I met them at the door, I asked Ron if he wanted a beer. He smiled and said no. Ron and Judy talked about their lives, their plans, and Jesus. I remember asking him a question: "Ron, you're a nice guy. You have everything going for you. Why would you want to be in ministry?" He did answer that. After my salvation, I learned of a comment Ron made to Judy after that first supper: "If God can save Ken Babington, He can save anyone". He did. He can. In fact, God has a Sovereign plan in motion for your salvation, life, and ministry.

FUNNY ASIDE: Cheryl took a pocket New Testament to the conference (March 5-7, 1976), and I took no Bible at all. After my silent conversation with the Lord, I became more attentive. In her teaching, Kay told everyone to turn to Psalm 1. I boldly, and loudly said, "I know where that is. It is right after Revelation". After the laughter died down, they explained about our pocket New Testament, with Psalms AFTER Revelation.

Allow me to follow that with two definitions. Ignorant is the lack of knowledge; uneducated. Stupid is showing carelessness, lacking interest, or appearing to have a lack of intelligence. I was just ignorant on where Psalm 1 is. No longer!

There is another part of my testimony that clearly shows the Sovereign hand of God in YOUR LIFE. Just after meeting Ron and Judy McIntosh, in early October, 1975 a close friend in the neighborhood, Tom Kime, asked me a question. Tom and his wife had a daughter the same age as our Lisa: five years old. Tom said he had just learned of an Episcopal church wanting to start a new church in our neighborhood. Tom and Thelma were like us: no desire to go to church. I told Tom: "We don't need it, but Lisa should start going to Sunday School. Tom, let's do it. We will be on the ground floor of this new church". His response shook me. He said, "There is one catch. We will need to attend a weekly Bible study every Thursday night". That was almost a deal breaker for both Tom and me. However, we reluctantly decided to go.

From October, 1975 until the end of February, 1976 (five months), we went to the Bible study and the weekly church service. To me, it was all boring. I did the weekly homework, but it meant nothing to me. In early January, 1976, the Bible study leaders began talking about a couple's conference/retreat in Chattanooga, Tennessee, in early March. It sounded interesting, and I thought it was going to be a camping trip. WRONG. The facilities were beautiful, and they had all the classes in an old red barn that had been made into a conference center. The keynote speaker was also the owner of the 32 acres, now known as Precept Ministries. Kay Arthur, her husband, Jack, several employees, along with her Associate Pastor, Bernie Kuiper, were the speakers. That weekend was my salvation, and my eternal destiny was resolved in that conference.

My life took a new direction that one weekend. When I left home, I was in the automobile business, on the way to owning my own Chrysler-Plymouth dealership. At age 29, my plan was to be financially able to retire at age 40. I returned home from that weekend conference with a new heart, a new mind-set, and a new-found passion for the Lord Jesus. I began my personal, in-depth study of the Bible, with no class, no training, and no assistance. On Wednesday morning, March 10, 1976, I attended the Precept class at Roswell Street Baptist. As I remember, there was one class for men, and 58 classes for women. After that class, I went into the church sanctuary, and sat in the front row, with 2,000 ladies, and a few men behind me. After the teaching by Kay, I was the first person to speak to her as she stood on the floor to talk. At that time, she knew nothing about me or my salvation. Within a minute she asked me to sit down and wait for her. At least half an hour later, she prayed with the last lady in line. She turned to me, and said "Walk with me downstairs". As we walked, we talked, and the friendship was anchored for life. As we got downstairs, we went into a room with 58 ladies, ready to be taught by Kay Arthur herself. I was the proverbial fly-on-the-wall, soaking it in like a new sponge. Each week, for almost 18 months, I attended the class; sat on the front row in the sanctuary; and went downstairs with Kay. Instead of sitting on the front row, after her pulpit teaching, within two weeks, I had a different vantage point. I went to the pulpit, worked with the sound guys, and then sat down by Kay's notes and her purse while she ministered at the altar. It was Kay Arthur who took that new convert with zero knowledge, and gave me study principles that she had developed. Kay had been discipled by Irving Jensen, and she taught me. By Monday, August 1, 1977, I was the full-time associate pastor of a Southern Baptist Church in Marietta, Georgia; and my family and I lived in the parsonage next door.

As an aside, I had a major decision to make, and for 45 years, I have wondered if I made the right decision. At the same time the church wanted to call me as associate pastor, Jack and Kay made Cheryl and me an offer. They wanted us to be the first married couple in their training class. I remember several details. First, they had no living quarters for a family. Second, I would have to work to support myself. We drove to Chattanooga, and looked for a home and a job. Instead, I agreed to the church position, with their blessing. For 45 years, I have wondered… what if…

Within 48 hours of my salvation, I was feebly studying the Bible at my desk, on my own, and that routine has only intensified and expanded since March, 1976. Here is another story to show me, really being ME. Jerry Lucas, retired NBA – Hall of Fame player, had a unique way to memorize entire Bible books. His conference was a week long, and I sat on the front row each night, maybe 1977. One night, I noticed my right shoe was black. I thought I had worn brown shoes, so I looked at my left shoe: BROWN. I was fashionably dressed for the front row in a memory conference. I still say "Hanging with me is never dull".

The reality of life, culture, and society changes, have been a small part of the WHY for this book. The absolute key WHY is really simple: I want to talk to you, the coming generations of leaders, about life. With a book, there is no distractions; no interruption; no misunderstanding; and nothing personal. Every reader reads the same words, so if you take something personal, that is between you and the

Lord. At that point, I caution you to listen, and heed His inner promptings. Now to the WHY.

I was raised in the most massive cultural change in America. World War II ended in victory for the U.S.A., and our nation has never really won another war since then. In reality, America has never fought to win since World War II. The military is ready. Politicians are not. The men and women who were in World War II were in their twenties and thirties when I was in elementary school (1952). I was a teenager when rock-n-roll bands began; when the hippie movement started; when draft-dodgers were my school mates; and when the drug culture began killing teenagers I knew. Then, in the military at age 19, I was one of those being yelled at by my peers who hated America as Americans. When I became an adult, it was my generation of political leaders who trashed our great nation inside Congress, and world-wide. John Kerry is barely two years older than me. Today, as a senior citizen who has always loved our country, I am one of the vast majority of Americans they want to get rid of so America can then "change". I have something to say to my family, and this book is one way I have selected to do it.

Introduction to Character Traits

Prior to Monday, August 1, 1977 (the exact date I began full time pastoral ministry), I had already heard of Bill Gothard, and his ministry to the Body of Christ. I had heard "about" the man, and the ministry, from both his friends and his foes. It really is amazing how splintered and divided the Body of Christ is on so many things. To my beloved family, I could shout it from a roof-top: Do not be part of division in the Body of Christ. There is no good end!!

I must take a side trip for a moment. I have numerous friends who disagree with me on doctrine. There is one pastor friend I have not seen in over 10 years. I have known him since 1985, and I would trust him without hesitation. He says God is NOT Sovereign. He is wrong, but that would never cause me to avoid him. In fact, if I heard he was in the hospital today, I would go visit him. All three of my children know this man, and I consider him a good friend. I implore my family to live out John 13:34, 35, and be NO PART of any schism or division, in the CHURCH. In 1 Corinthians 12:25, we are to have the same care one for another, without schism!! Now, back to Character Traits, our topic.

It was in 1979 when I attended my first ALL DAYS PASTOR'S SEMINAR with Bill Gothard. There may have been around 2,000 pastors in attendance, and I remember leaving with enthusiasm in what I had heard, learned, and received. From that day until today as I write this, I have trusted Bill Gothard and his ministry. Bill and I exchange emails today, and I respect the man and his ministry! Just one small aspect of his ministry is the Character Traits. He developed 49 separate traits, and he has written extensively about those traits. His presentation is professional, Biblical, and extremely practical. Many years ago, I received his permission to use the character traits, and I promised him I would always credit him. I will never hesitate to acknowledge the wisdom and ministry of Bill Gothard in my life!!

Before getting to the character traits themselves, I must give you a brief Bible study on "express image". My favorite dictionary is the 1828 American Dictionary, by Noah Webster. Yes, I have a hard-bound copy on my desk. Our English word "character" comes from the Greek word (#5481 in Strong's) χαρακτήρ. That Greek word has a fascinating definition. In the Strong's, it is an exact copy, representation. In Thayer's, that Greek word is the instrument used in engraving/carving. It is the mark stamped upon that instrument. It is a mark stamped or burned into. It is the precise reproduction in every respect. In the Vine's Expository Dictionary, that word is defined as a tool for graving; to cut into; a stamp/impress, as on a coin. According to Dr. Vine, the object stamped bears the image of the seal used to stamp on an object. Then, Dr. Vine's concludes with: "All features of the object correspond respectively with those of the instrument, seal". More below! Noah Webster, in his #4 definition of "character" says: character is the peculiar qualities, impressed by nature or habit on a person, which distinguish him from others. So far, for this book, we have a fascinating definition of "character" from Noah Webster, and the Greek word that brought us our English word. It is now time for the spiritual right-hook, knock out punch.

The Greek word, χαρακτή, is used in the Bible, 2,000 years ago. It is only used once in the entire Bible. If you were reading the King James, you would most likely read Hebrews 1:3 without a clue how **AMAZING** that verse is. It says Jesus is "the express image of His person...". Jesus is the express image of God. The exact Greek word used by the Holy Spirit 2,000 years ago, with the writer of Hebrews; used to describe Jesus; is translated "express image" in Hebrews 1:3; the ONLY TIME that Greek word is used in the Bible. It is time for spiritual meat on this spiritual bone.

Dr. Vine wrote about Hebrews 1:3 in his expository dictionary as he defined the Greek word χαρακτήρ, used to give us the English word, CHARACTER. From Dr. Vine about "express image" in Hebrews 1:3 – the Son is personally distinct from, and yet literally equal to God, whose essence, Jesus, is the adequate imprint. Jesus is the image, impress of God's substance or essence. It is the complete similarity which this word stresses. Case closed? NO WAY. Here is the official K.O. (knock out) punch.

First, a disclaimer. A pastor recently told me I should not make the following comment because it could lead to improper application. His reasoning was based on writings of current theologians and their commentaries on Hebrews 1:3. I listened to his reasoning and went to the Lord in serious prayer. My conclusion was simple, clear, and convincing to me. A commentary is the written belief of the author of that commentary. I appreciate A.W. Pink commentaries. Matthew Henry has written an entire Bible commentary. Oliver Greene wrote fabulous commentaries. One man, William Barclay (1907-1978), wrote well over 75 books and most likely over 80% of pastors in America have at least one of his commentaries in their library. William Barclay was a heretic. He denied the inerrancy. He denied the Virgin Birth. He denied the miracles of Jesus, and he denied the substitutionary death of Jesus. In Bible College, I wrote a 21 page report on Barclay, and quoted his words 57 times. My professor took my report to the College book store, and every one of his books was removed. So this is NOT an opinion!! Almost without exception, virtually every pastor I have spoken to about Barclay says they know his theology is off-base, but "he is excellent on Greek and geography". A little rat poison in the hamburger does not make it acceptable and palatable. To my loving family, YOU MUST GUARD TRUTH. STUDY THE WORD.

As I prayed on the pastor's comment to me, my answer became clear. His decision was based on commentaries, written by men. My decision was based 100% on the Greek word selected by the Holy Spirit, as defined, without commentary. Therefore, the next paragraph is written by me, to my family members, with

Biblical confidence, and accurate practical application, using ONLY the word (character) used by the Holy Spirit in the written content of Hebrews 1:3. Whew. Now, buckle up.

As you read and consider the following Character Traits, remember this: around 65 AD, when Hebrews was written, the Holy Spirit selected the Greek word, χαρακτήρ, (2 Peter 1:20, 21) to be written in what we know as Hebrews 1:3, now translated in the KJV as "express image". Many translations use "character", and the Greek word itself is CHARACTER. Get ready. It is time for the knockout punch.

As a Christian, you have Jesus living inside you, by His Holy Spirit. In most verses, we Christians are "in Jesus". In Galatians 2:20, Colossians 1:27, Philemon 1:6, and others, Jesus is IN YOU, the believer. In Colossians 3:1-4, your life is hid with Christ, in God. From 2 Corinthians 5:17 and Colossians 2:6, we are in Christ. There are over 75 verses that confirm Christians are **in Jesus**. When Jesus was with His disciples for the last time before His crucifixion, He told them of the Ministry of the Holy Spirit (John 14, 15, 16). Look at John 14:16-18; 14:26, 27; John 15:26, 27; John 16:7; 16:13-15, and more. As a Christian, you are IN JESUS, and Jesus is IN you.

THEREFORE, based on the inerrant Word of God, as a Christian, with Jesus in you, you have the "express image"; you have **THE "CHARACTER" OF GOD** living inside you. Think about that as you review the following Character Traits. Our English word character, comes from the Greek word character; used only once in the Bible (Hebrews 1:3); referring to Jesus being the character of God; and this Jesus, the character of God, lives within you. From an accurate Biblical perspective, you, as a Christian, have the character of God living within you. Any description about character traits can be traced back to Jesus, the express image, character, of God, who lives in you every day.

I have always loved Philippians 1:6 and Philemon 1:6. As you ponder (Intentional! I love you, Ponder-Sissy!) the Character Traits, always know His character (Jesus) was implanted inside you at salvation. May I exhort you to let Jesus guide your daily life to please Him (John 16:33).

Now, to the Character Traits:

ALERTNESS vs. unawareness – Mark 14:38

Ability to anticipate right responses to that which is taking place around me.

Be aware of your surroundings

Be on a personal "high alert" regarding your surroundings

Be vigilant and watchful

This alertness takes place before you know the actual need

ATTENTIVENESS vs. unconcern – Hebrews 2:1

To be a good listener

To be observant to your surroundings

A good driver is attentive

Pay attention

You can train yourself to do this

AVAILABILITY vs. self-centeredness – Philippians 2:19-21

You see an unmet need

You know you are competent to meet the need

You have the time and physical energy

It could be family, friend, or stranger

The need gets accomplished because of you

BOLDNESS vs. fearfulness – Acts 4:29

Confidence that what I have to say or do is true, right, and just, in the sight of God.

Courage and bravery

Exceeding ordinary expectations

You are fearless and confident in your ability, tactics, and results

You proceed, knowing 1 John 4:4

CAUTIOUSNESS vs. rashness – Proverbs 19:2

Knowing how important right timing is in accomplishing right actions

Watch with a desire to avoid harm or danger

Proceed carefully

Like President Reagan: "Trust, but verify"

You do keep going!

COMPASSION vs. indifference – 1 John 3:17

Investing whatever is necessary to heal the hurts of others

Like the Indian saying: "May I never judge another man until I have walked a mile in his moccasins."

You suffer with the other person

You put yourself in their shoes

You comfort them, and want to help them

You might become their advocate/answer

You do become their friend

CONTENTMENT vs. covetousness – 1 Timothy 6:8, Psalm 37:25 and Hebrews 13:5, 6

Realizing that God has provided everything I need for my present happiness

Peace of mind, regardless of…

CREATIVITY vs. underachievement – Romans 12:2

Approaching a need, a task, an idea, from a new perspective

You sense a need with an opportunity

You begin to think of a possible answer, solution for the need

You think, take notes, develop a plan, and implement

Your creativity starts in your mind, heart

DECISIVENESS vs. double-mindedness – James 1:5

The ability to finalize difficult decisions based on the will and ways of God

You know the right and proper answer

You are able to make the final decision

You are willing to step out, trusting the Lord

You put an end to controversy

Final and conclusive

You now proceed to your God given duty with confidence

DEFERENCE vs. rudeness – Romans 14:21

Limiting my freedom in order not to offend the priorities of those whom God has called me to serve

This is the ability and desire to yield to others

Your decision to yield will benefit the one to whom you yield

There is no personal gain to the one who yields

DEPENDABILITY vs. inconsistency – Psalm 15:4

Fulfilling what I consented to do even if it means unexpected personal sacrifices

To be reliable when needed, or when there is a need

This is a consistent character trait

You build a reputation for a proven track-record

You are a man of your word

It is as if you are attached to the need, with a desire to accomplish the task to be done

DETERMINATION vs. faintheartedness – 2 Timothy 4:7-8

Purposing to accomplish God's goals, in God's time, regardless of opposition

This is a firm resolution with an absolute direction

You have a "no quit" mindset

You are not a slacker, not a sluggard

It is as if you mentally say : "Every glass is half full"

You are not slothful

You continue to do what needs to be done

DILIGENCE vs. slothfulness – Colossians 3:23

Visualizing each task as a special assignment from the Lord, using all my energy to accomplish it.

A task is undone, and someone needs to "step-up"

You do the constant effort in WHAT, HOW needs are to be done

There is no "wait", "later", "no", procrastination

The need is met quickly and efficiently

DISCERNMENT vs. judgment – 1 Samuel 16:7

The God-given ability to understand why things happen; or why they MAY happen

This is knowledge without factually KNOWING

You see past what the eyes see or do not see

You distinguish in your mind first

Some people refer to this as "a gut feeling"

This is doing, without being prejudice or judgmental

DISCRETION vs. simplemindedness – Proverbs 22:3

The ability to avoid words, actions, and attitudes which could result in undesirable consequences.

The ability and desire to keep a secret

Not being prone to gossip

You keep known information out of the public domain

You NEVER use knowledge of others for personal gain

You judge internally what is right and proper

You keep things quiet and private

ENDURANCE vs. giving up – Galatians 6:9

The inward strength to withstand stress to accomplish God's best

In a marathon, runners hit "the wall". They either quit, or they endure to the finish line.

Endurance is a never quit mindset

You pace yourself to finish properly

You continue regardless of pain and suffering

ENTHUSIASM vs. apathy – 1 Thessalonians 5:16-19

Expressing with my soul the joy of my spirit

This begins internally, regardless of circumstances or reality itself

It is a confident pursuit of what is right

The 1828 Noah Webster Dictionary says this is to infuse a Divine Spirit

Our English word comes from the Greek: "IN God"

Your enthusiasm is a source of inner strength for others

FAITH vs. presumption – Hebrews 11:1

Visualizing what God intends to do in a given situation, and acting in harmony with Him.

A calm assurance to proceed

It is based on "tested - proven" of the unseen/unknown

With believers, our faith is in His inerrant Word to us

Faith produces an allegiance to duty, because this duty is RIGHT

FLEXIBILITY vs. resistance – Colossians 3:2

Not setting my affections on ideas or plans which could be changed by God or others

Example: A stubborn person is the one who does not do what I want them to do. **THINK THROUGH THAT!!**

Easily able to change my opinion, direction

Not rigid, and instead, teachable with TRUTH

Ability to discuss, listen, and possibly bend

Flexibility must always be toward truth

FORGIVENESS vs. rejection – Ephesians 4:32

Clearing the record of those who have wronged me, and allowing God to love them through me

To pardon the offender with the desire to be restored: God does this with you

This brings a sense of healing to the offender

When you need to apologize, do it quickly

When someone apologizes to you, be reconciled without bringing the offense up

GENEROSITY vs. stinginess – 2 Corinthians 9:6

Realizing that all I have belongs to God, and using it for His purpose

Liberal giving, without constraint, reward, or personal benefit

It is usually thought of as financial

It could be time, counsel, protection, defending

You see the need, and you proceed without concern for the personal cost to you

Your generosity will be an appreciated blessing to others

GENTLENESS vs. harshness – 1 Thessalonians 2:7

Showing personal care and concern in meeting the need of others

This is a mild-mannered temperament

A mother alligator uses this when she places her newborn babies in her mouth

You would use this if you were in a race, holding an unbroken egg in a spoon

The desire to NOT BE rude, harsh, or brazen

GRATEFULNESS vs. unthankfulness – 1 Corinthians 4:7

Making known appreciation to God and others for the ways they have benefited my life

Gratitude to the Lord, and to people

Sincere thankfulness for what others have done in your life and spiritual growth

This includes vertical toward God, and horizontal toward people who have helped you

Your "thank you" shows appreciation as the receiver

An interesting passage is 1 Thessalonians 2:19, 20. We take people with us into eternity.

GRATITUDE vs. unthankfulness – 1 Corinthians 4:7

Making known to God and others in what ways they have benefited my life

Same Character Trait as GRATEFULNESS

HOSPITALITY vs. loneliness – Hebrews 13:2

Cheerfully sharing food, shelter, and spiritual refreshment with those God brings into my life

The desire to receive and entertain people without expectation of personal reward or benefit

No hidden agenda!!

Open up what is yours, to benefit others

An eagerness with no rush to end

HUMILITY vs. pride – James 4:6

Recognizing that it is God and others who are responsible for the achievements in my life

You see the intrinsic value and goodness of others over your own

"Others first" - JOY: Jesus, others, you

A modest appraisal of yourself, kept to yourself

Freedom from pride or arrogance

Easily accessible to others

INITIATIVE vs. unresponsiveness – Romans 12:21

Recognizing and doing what needs to be done before I am asked to do it

Illustration: "Prime the pump" - "snowball effect"

Initiative is: YOU do the first - get it started

Do not wait to be asked, told

You do what is needed because it is needed to be done

Your initiative may create initiative in others

JOYFULNESS vs. self-pity – Psalm 16:11 and Proverbs 15:13

The spontaneous enthusiasm of my spirit, when my soul is in fellowship with the Lord

You are the life of the party

You are joyful, regardless of…

You are NOT downtrodden, or on a pity party

You rejoice in Jesus

Like Teflon, nothing sticks to you to discourage you

You are comfortable inside you

You have an expectation of exhilaration in you

JUSTICE vs. fairness – Micah 6:8

Personal responsibility to God's unchanging laws

Justice is based on a truthful standard

Justice is in line with God given laws

There is no partiality or judgmental attitude

This standard is equal without unjust "equality"

This standard is based on law, not fairness

Justice cannot be bought or bribery

Justice is everyone receiving as they are due, based on laws

KINDNESS vs. rudeness - Ephesians 4:32

The desire, with follow-through, to show appreciation toward others, by word or deed

This is extended to individuals without partiality

This may be a "random act of kindness"

This is a natural habit – who you are!

You delight in contributing to the contentment of others

Just be nice!

LOVE vs. selfishness – 1 Corinthians 13:3

Giving to others' basic needs without having any motive for personal reward

Love is who you are: a noun

Loves is how you live: a verb

It is easy to "love" a nice person

True LOVE is directed toward the unlovely

LOVE extends to your enemies, those who hate you, and persecute you

LOYALTY vs. unfaithfulness – John 15:13

Demonstrate my commitment to God and to those whom He has called me to serve.

Please keep $5 million for 10 years. Ten years later, same exact serial numbers!

Faithful, fidelity

A loyal person is not a fair weather friend

True loyalty is both rare and priceless, solidified over time

MEEKNESS vs. anger – Psalm 62:5

Yielding my personal rights and expectations to God

Proverbs 17:28 explains this trait

Controlled strength in the face of opposition

Meekness is most certainly NOT weakness

Fearless, mild mannered temper

Forbearance under personal pain or injury

OBEDIENCE vs. willfulness – 2 Corinthians 10:5

Freedom to be creative under the protection of divinely appointed authority

A willing and immediate compliance

It could be a request, order, command, or instruction

Again, it is an immediate compliance

Parents should teach "first time obedience"

A willingness to submit to individuals or an authority

A willingness to set your own priorities aside for the benefit of another person

ORDERLINESS vs. disorganization – 1 Corinthians 14:40

Preparing myself and my surroundings so I will achieve the greatest efficiency.

A methodical, organized, planned life

You do not need to be a perfectionist

You are not "OCD - Obsessive Compulsive Disorder"

You are like a well-oiled machine

This creates a smooth running lifestyle with purpose

Orderliness extends to all areas of life

PATIENCE vs. restlessness – Romans 5:3, 4

Accepting a difficult situation from God without giving Him a deadline to remove it

The desire to continue, unruffled, despite…

Perseverance under pressure and problems

The inner ability to endure and persist

PERSUASIVENESS vs. contentiousness – 2 Timothy 2:24-26

Guiding vital truths around another's mental roadblocks

The ability to make your point with sensible reasons and presentation

Ability to present details with truth and conviction

Ability to influence others to your side

PUNCTUALITY vs. tardiness – Ecclesiastes 3:1

Showing high esteem for other people and their time

It is better to be 30 minutes early, rather than one minute late

Punctually usually extends to TIME

It could include appointments, debt payment, and more

This is illustrated by keeping accurate records

Shows time management skills

Shows responsibility

RESOURCEFULNESS vs. wastefulness – Luke 16:10

Wise use of that which others would normally overlook or discard.

You become the "go to guy"

You have the ability to find resources for…

The television show MacGyver is an excellent illustration

"Radar" on the television show M.A.S.H. was resourceful

You become the person entrusted to accomplish the given task, mission

RESPONSIBILITY vs. unreliability – Romans 14:12

Knowing and doing what both God and others are expecting from me.

This is a combination of numerous traits

You act and speak because you are accountable to God

You act because you are answerable to God

You act because it is the right thing to do

It is the eager discharge of your obligation

REVERENCE vs. disrespect – Proverbs 23:18-23

Awareness of how God is working through people and to produce the character of Christ in me.

This trait shows respect for authority

You esteem the value of another person

You act sincerely, respectfully, with appreciation

You act by holding another person on a "pedestal"

SECURITY vs. anxiety – John 6:27

Structuring my life around that which is eternal, and cannot be destroyed or taken away.

Know you are guarded and protected by an outside source: God

You are safe, insulated, untouchable, by a trusted source greater than you: God

This trait produces freedom and confidence

SELF-CONTROL vs. self-indulgence – Galatians 5:24-25

Instant obedience to the initial promptings of God's Spirit.

"The end justifies the means" ignores, invalidates, and is a disgrace to self-control

This exemplifies self-discipline to do what is proper

Self-control begins with a decision in your mind

It is the ability to say NO, for the greater good

SENSITIVITY vs. callousness – Romans 12:15

Exercising my senses so I can perceive the true spirit and emotions of those around me

Moved by the needs of others

You have a perceived impression from an outside source: God

He leads you to action on behalf of the one in need

SINCERITY vs. hypocrisy – 1 Peter 1:22

Eagerness to do what is right, with transparent motives

In Bible times, a person would hold a plate toward the sun. If it had been cracked and glued, the sunlight would show the flaw. If there was no flaw from that direct sunlight, the plate was "sine-sere" – sincere!

Without blemish

Honest intentions

Free from hypocrisy, false pretense, bad motives

THOROUGHNESS vs. incompleteness – Proverbs 18:15

Knowing what factors will diminish the effectiveness of my work or words if neglected

Details to their entirety

Complete, full, with precision

Not just surface details

Phrase: "If something is worth doing, it is worth doing right".

THRIFTINESS vs. extravagance – Luke 16:11

Not letting myself or others spend that which is not necessary

Good management of resources for economic benefit

Being frugal is much different than being cheap

With this trait, you are frugal with your resources, so you will be able to meet the needs of others.

TOLERANCE vs. prejudice – Philippians 2:2

Accepting others as unique expressions of specific character qualities in varying degrees of maturity.

To allow the freedom of people to choose

To allow the freedom of opinion for others

You will not force your opinion on others

You are willing to keep unity, especially in disagreement

Phrase: "I may disagree with you, but I will fight to my death for your freedom to decide".

TRUTHFULNESS vs. deception – Ephesians 4:25

Earning future trust by accurately reporting past facts.

By simple definition, it means "full of truth"

Honesty under pressure

Speaking while under oath in your mind

There is no need for a lie-detector

A phrase: salesman says: "I will tell you the truth…" Customer: "Do you normally lie?"

Speak truth as a habit

VIRTUE vs. impurity – 2 Peter 1:3-5

The moral excellence and purity of spirit that radiate from my life as I obey God's Word.

Brave

Valor

Moral goodness

Living in conformity with moral expectations, laws, and duty

WISDOM vs. natural inclinations – Proverbs 9:10

Seeing and responding to life's situations from God's frame of reference

Colossians 2:3 – All the treasures of WISDOM are hidden in Christ Jesus

Putting knowledge to practical application

The right and proper use of knowledge

Sound judgment based on true facts

Wisdom guides you in the correct direction of life

ZEAL – Titus 2:14

Our English word ZEAL, comes from the Greek word ζῆλος (#2205 – Strong's)

That Greek word means:

Hot – heat – excitement of mind

Fervor in spirit – uncompromising partisan

Ardor in embracing, pursuing, defending anything

Passionate pursuit

Leads to enthusiasm

When you are eager to do and accomplish

Nothing hinders you

Beloved family members, I do have a thorough study with over 50 separate, individual Character Traits. As you work to refine these traits in you, others will know you as their priceless friend for life.

CHARACTER TRAITS CONCLUSION

While the above title says you are now at the Conclusion, that is a misnomer. The title could be: Introduction, Part 2, or The Beginning. This has not been a study that you now say is done, so I can set it aside and move on. NO WAY. Just the opposite. It is not like you have "arrived". Instead, you have the tools to get to your destination. If you received a ladder and roofing shingles, you would not have a new roof. You would have the ingredients for a new roof. The one thing that is needed for a new roof is: WORK. You, beloved, supply the manual labor for character.

There is both a comparison and contrast with Character Traits and Spiritual Gifts. Both can be used, abused, or ignored. Spiritual Gifts are only for believers, and every believer, without exception, has at least one. You may have more than one, but you most certainly have one, at a minimum. These gifts are to be used primarily inside the Church, the Body of Christ. Yes, I do have a thorough study on Spiritual Gifts. Character Traits are different. They are traits that can be used by Christians, non-Christians, atheists, agnostics, or non-religious people. Both are beneficial to the recipient, and there is an almost fool-proof formula for an effective life and ministry, using the Character Traits. In life, people are almost universally familiar with "The Golden Rule". That is a Bible principle from Leviticus 19, Matthew 7:12, and expanded in Matthew 22:34-40. As you apply the Golden Rule in virtually every situation, during every moment, of every day, from every month, and every year, you will be a walking, breathing, poster board for Character Traits. Look at each individual character. Almost without exception, they involve other people. Would you like people to be kind to you? Be kind! Character. And so it goes.

We will conclude Character Traits with one more comparison between Spiritual Gifts and Character Traits. First, you, individually, and personally, are responsible. The Lord has given you specific Character Traits, and you are responsible. When you treat people the way you want to be treated, you are absolutely using Character Traits. When you refuse to treat others the way you would want them to treat you, you are then being irresponsible. You and I are RESPONSIBLE. There is a second prong here. As Christians, there will be a day in the future, as described in 2 Corinthians 5:10. That principle is also referred to in

Matthew 16:27; Acts 10:42; Romans 2:16; Romans 14:10 and 14:12; and in Ephesians 6:8. Simply put, the principle goes like this: you are accountable. As a Christian, there will be a day in the future, when you give an accounting of your very life, to the One who died for you. Good news: that accounting has ZERO to do with salvation, and everything to do with rewards after you are dead. Bad news: you are responsible now, with those same rewards only given after your life on earth is complete, finished, and in the record book.

Here is loving counsel to my family. Treat people the way you want people to treat you. It really is that basic, and there is a natural conclusion. You will quickly build a name and reputation for yourself. People will talk about you, and how amazingly nice you are. People will talk about your character, without a clue you are treating them the same way you would want them to treat you, based on CHARACTER. Try that. You will enjoy it.

Stand beside a calm, glass-surface lake, with a crystal clear reflection. It is a beautiful scene. Next, pick up a pebble from the ground, and throw it in the water. A ripple effect begins to spread out across the lake. Your Matthew 7:12 lifestyle will create the same type of spiritual ripple. Back to the lake. If you took a small pebble, and threw it to skip over the surface of the water, you would create multiple ripple effects. That, my family, will be the result of your consistent lifestyle of character. I urge you to start today, with a non-stop attitude until you meet Jesus face-to-face. I can assure you, based on His Word: If you do these as a habit, routine, then you will most certainly hear that "well done" (Matthew 25:21) from the One who died for you.

Start today!

I love you…
Paw Paw

A BOY NAMED GEORGE

I had several options as I did my "due-diligence" research, on this one, with no rigid guarantee. So, I will speculate with absolute rigid accuracy. What you are about to read was written by a young man, when he was between 13-16 years old – guaranteed! Most sources say he was 14 when he wrote the following.

George Washington (February 22, 1732 – December 14, 1799) had a favorite book before he was a teenager. He read, re-read, studied, used, and abused the book, and took that one book to heart in his daily life. The book was entitled "The Young Man's Companion", written in London in 1664. By the time he was around 14 years old, George

Washington had developed his own "rules", and at that age, young George wrote his own book. He titled it "Rules for Civility and Decent Behavior" – age 14!! This book became his own "go-to" book since he wrote it. Summed up, the teenager established his own set of guidelines and parameters for civility. To summarize, it would be: be kind; respectful; polite; discreet; humble, and more. Have good table manners. Show courtesy to all. Be a servant to all. Be modest in your dress code and conversations. In his own words, young George Washington wrote 110 rules for civility and decent behavior. Rule #6 is excellent. Rule #9 says: do not spit into a fire, especially if someone is cooking meat. Rule #38 is do not play the doctor when visiting the sick. And so they go: 110 rules for civility and decent behavior, written by 14 year old George Washington.

As you read these rules, written over 250 ago (1746), they are practical for you today. Enjoy them; embrace them; make them yours; and may the Lord continue to etch His character into your daily life.

1. When you are with people, always do everything with respect to others.
2. When with others, do not put your hands on your own body improperly.
3. Show nothing to your friend that may frighten him.
4. When with others, do not sing to yourself, hum, or drum your fingers.
5. If you cough, sneeze, or yawn, do it discreetly.
6. Rules of personal etiquette:
    - ✓ Do not sleep when others speak
    - ✓ Do not sit when others stand
    - ✓ Do not speak when you should hold your peace

- ✓ Do not keep walking when others stop
7. Do not undress in the company of others. Also, do not be half-dressed while with others.
8. Give respect to each individual person.
9. Do not spit into a fire. Do not warm your hands or feet in a fire, especially if there is meat on the fire.
10. When you sit down, do not cross your legs, or put one leg on the other.
11. Do not shift yourself in the sight of others, nor gnaw your fingernails.
12. Do not shake your head; roll your eyes; lift one eyebrow higher; make any "face", nor spit when approaching someone.
13. Do not kill fleas, ticks, lice, in the presence of others. Be discreet when removing particles from your clothes.
14. Do not turn your back on someone speaking. Do not shake the table when someone is reading or writing. Do not lean on anyone.
15. Keep your nails short and clean. Keep your hands and teeth clean.
16. Do not puff up your cheeks, stick your tongue out, or bite your lips.
17. Do not be a flatterer, and do not be rude.
18. Do not read in the presence of others, and if necessary, step into another room. Also, do not read over the shoulder of another person.
19. Let your countenance be pleasant, yet serious in grave situations.
20. Your body gestures must be suited to your discourse.
21. Reproach none for infirmities of nature, nor delight to put them down that have in mind thereof.

22. Show not yourself glad at the misfortune of another, though he were your enemy.
23. Always show pity to the suffering offender in his punishment, even if you are inwardly pleased.
24. Do not laugh too loud or too much at any public spectacle.
25. Superfluous compliments, and all effect of ceremonies are to be avoided, yet where they are due, do not neglect them.
26. Remove your hat and bow with respect to people of distinction.
27. Be cautious of your hat when you salute.
28. If someone speaks to you while you are seated, stand up to give attention as you listen.
29. Give way to others as they approach you, or the door.
30. Place yourself on the left side of people with honor. If three walk together, the more honorable goes in the middle. The wall, or inside, is given to the more honorable.
31. Be respectful in giving place to others.
32. Give priority to other people in lodging.
33. Those of dignity or office should be given priority.
34. It is good manners to allow others to speak before you.
35. When in business, speak briefly, with comprehension.
36. Be respectful of all people: higher or lower than you.
37. When speaking to men of quality, keep at least a pace away, and do not lean into them.
38. Do not play physician when visiting the sick.
39. Give due title to those you write or speak to.

40. Do not argue with your superior.
41. Do not attempt to "teach" someone in their own profession. That savors of arrogancy.
42. Let your courtesy be proper. Do not act the same with a clown and a prince.
43. Do not express joy with someone in pain.
44. Do not blame a man who does all he can do, even if it may not succeed.
45. Be very cautious and discreet when you reprove anyone.
46. Take all admonitions thankfully.
47. Mock not, nor jest at anything of importance. Be cautious with sarcasm, and do not laugh at what you said.
48. Be unblameable when you reprove others.
49. Do not curse or revile others.
50. Do not quickly believe gossip.
51. Be neat and presentable in how you dress.
52. Be modest in your apparel; show respect.
53. Do not act as if you are crazy in public.
54. Do not play like a peacock, showing off what you wear.
55. Eat not in the street, nor out of season.
56. Associate with men of good quality. It is better to be alone than in bad company.
57. Walk beside others, always giving respect to them.
58. Let your conversation be without malice or envy.
59. Never act against the rules of moral behavior to those inferior to you.
60. Do not be immodest in urging your friends to discover a secret.
61. Be cautious and respectful in all your conversations.

62. Be cautious in "how" you talk respectfully to others.
63. Do not be prideful or arrogant regarding yourself.
64. Do not deride any man's misfortune.
65. Never speak injurious words; even if given the opportunity.
66. Always be first to show respect and courtesy.
67. Do not be demanding or detract from others.
68. Do not give advice when not asked; when asked, be brief in your advice.
69. Do not be demanding in your opinion. Show preference to others.
70. Do not speak of the frailties of others.
71. Do not gaze at the marks, blemishes, or imperfections of others.
72. Do not speak in an unknown tongue in company.
73. Think before you speak, and pronounce words properly.
74. Be attentive when others speak. Do not interrupt, but if they hesitate to remember a word, help them discreetly.
75. Do not interrupt others when they speak.
76. Do not point your finger at the person to whom you speak.
77. Do not whisper in the company of others.
78. Make no comparisons, and do not commend another, when someone is being honored.
79. Do not gossip, and do not give away secrets.
80. Do not be tedious in discourse or reading, unless the company enjoys it.
81. Do not interrupt people speaking in private.
82. Do not promise what you cannot deliver. Keep your promise.

83. When you deliver a matter, do it without passion or discretions, even if the recipient is mean.
84. When your superior is talking to someone else, do not attempt to listen in.
85. Do not speak unless you are asked. Even then, stand up, speak clearly, respectfully, and briefly!
86. In disputes, do not demand your opinion.
87. Do not be argumentative.
88. Do not be repetitive in your discourse.
89. Do not speak evil of a person not there.
90. When eating, do not scratch, spit, or blow you nose.
91. Your table manners show your true character.
92. Take no salt or cut bread with a greasy knife.
93. Be polite and respectful to others at your table as you dine.
94. If you put your bread in broth, let it be no more than one mouthful at a time.
95. Do not eat your meat with your knife in your hand.
96. When eating, keep your hands clean.
97. Do not put more food into your mouth until you swallow.
98. Do not talk or drink with your mouth full.
99. Before and after you drink, wipe your lips.
100. Do not use the tablecloth to clean your hands or your teeth.
101. Do not rinse your mouth in the presence of others.
102. Do not eat or drink with the same people often.
103. Do not be the last person to finish eating. Also, do not put your arm on the table.
104. Allow the senior person to eat first!
105. Do not get angry at the table, even if that anger is warranted.

106. Do not automatically sit at the head seat at the table.
107. Be attentive to others speaking, and do not speak with food in your mouth.
108. When you speak of God, let it be seriously and with reverence. Honor and obey your parents, even if they are poor.
109. Let your recreations be manful, not sinful.
110. Labor to keep alive in your breast that little spark of celestial fire called conscience!

CONCLUSION

You may have smiled as you read these, but NO ONE, anywhere, had any idea that the teenager who penned these rules would be a strategic military genius; our first President; and remembered as "The Father of America". We, today, know that in hindsight. What will people say about you 100 years from now? That is totally dependent on the way you live today. May 1 Corinthians 15:57, 58 refer to you.

UNSOLICITED COUNSEL

Speaking generically, children typically do not understand the complete ROLL of their parents. Most children nationwide do not see, value, or appreciate the true ministry of their parents. In the NASB, in 1 Thessalonians 2, Paul said he was like a gentle nursing mother, tenderly caring for her children (verse 7); and imploring as a father would his own children (verse 11). The result was in verse 12:
"...that ye would walk worthy of God, Who hath called you unto His kingdom and glory". There are numerous other verses, but Paul's words in Thessalonians 2 are interesting.

For your reading, you might want to review Deuteronomy 6:4-9; Joshua 24:14, 15; and Judges 2:10 (a very sad verse!); Malachi 4:6; and Ephesians 6:1-4. I have a study on Proverbs and the Family; but suffice it to say: your parents have an extremely important spiritual function in your life.

Since I am 76, I have a lot of friends I say are "over 60". Recently, I sent out an email and did in-person sessions with friends, specifically for this book. My instructions were simple: you have a small group of teenagers for a few minutes. What non-spiritual life counsel would you give them? Now, back to my family. As you read the following, your age is immaterial. There is nothing to be taken "personal" to you, other than the Holy Spirit Himself working in you. These thoughts are in no order, and these are just a small sample of the answers I received. Here is how I suggest you read this section. First, read each one slowly, without a concern for finishing quickly. Digest each individual point. As you read, I want you to have two thoughts in mind CONSTANTLY.

How am I doing on this one thing right now, today?

As a parent myself, would I want my children to follow this counsel?

With over 45 years of pastoral ministry, I have seen and heard many stories. I have performed weddings for people who are now biological grandparents! I have witnessed rude, obnoxious, rebellious children grow up, scolding their own children for acting the same way that parent did as a child. The following is given to my family from total strangers, and grandparents. That means this counsel is coming from the "older baby boomers" (1945-1965), and the younger "silent generation (1928-1945). These men and women have decades of life-experience, and I submit their thoughts to you as words of wisdom from the school of life. Here we go, again: in no order, and absolutely nothing personal.

The bold points are from strangers. The brief commentary is from me! I love you.

1. **Be resilient**
   Remember, I did not intentionally start with this, but it is an excellent starting point. The word "resilient" means to leap-back, spring-back, rebound, and start-back. In life, you will always have issues or people that hurt you in some way (usually emotionally, inside you!). Do not let those people be in charge of you by remote control. Ignore them, and bounce back into life.
2. **Build a good foundation**
   On March 27, 1981, in Cocoa Beach, Florida, 11 people were killed while building a five story condominium (Harbor Cay Condominium). The cause was discovered to be intentional by faulty workmanship: the concrete foundation had been diluted to increase the profit: a bad foundation. Build your life with the rock-solid foundation of the Lord Jesus Christ.
3. **Do not be judgmental**
   I guarantee, all people, for all your life, will not agree with you 100%. Guaranteed! You will meet people who think, dress, and talk different than you. These are the people you will witness to about Jesus. Do not be judgmental.
4. **Be victorious, not a victim**
   That is an interesting thought. At some point, regardless how minor, you will be a victim. I remember our home was broken into when Lisa was

about five years old. Being a victim must not define you. The Bible says so much about you being more than a conqueror, and triumphant (Romans 8:37-39 and 2 Corinthians 2:14).

5. **Love people**
There is no one better-than-you, nor is there anyone beneath you. I have repeatedly said "you only have one chance at a first impression". When you truly love people, you look past their frailties, and you intentionally work to make them better, with their appreciation. Proverbs 17:28 is a good place to start loving people.

6. **Do not yield to peer-pressure**
You will always have bullies who appear to be brazen and demanding. When people demean you for not "joining" with them, it may well be due to their desire to use you with improper motives. Check out my friend, Quartavious Davis (Federal prison ID: #96427-004). He was born in 1991, and at age 19, yielded to peer-pressure. Within months, he was arrested. No one was hurt, and his friends turned against him. Quartavious will be released from Federal prison on September 15, 2147!! I implore you: do not yield to peer-pressure.

7. **Enjoy good music**
I am a bad one on this topic, because I am not a music guy. I cannot understand the words as the song is sung, and the music itself is not usually melodious for me. However, most people love music. Be cautious. The noise itself will affect your ears. The rhythm affects your emotions, and the words get into your brain for thinking, possibly leading to improper

action. I suggest you learn praise choruses. You will love them, and they will draw you to worship Jesus.

8. **Pursue your talents**

    You do have God given talents. Use them, and watch what the Lord will do in your life. My brother-in-law, Keith Shook, was doing electrical wiring in the garage, at age seven. I was there watching him! At age five, Keith Thibodeaux was selected to play "little Ricky" on "I Love Lucy". At age five, he was proficient on the drums. No one knew that years later, he and his wife Kathy would have a ministry known as "Ballet Magnificat". Pursue your God-given talents. You have those talents for His glory.

9. **Keep your mind from evil thoughts**

    Life will always start in your head, prompted by your heart. Read Proverbs 4:23 and 23:26. In Genesis 3:6, Eve saw the tree...; in Joshua 7:21, Achan saw; in 2 Samuel 11:2, David saw Bathsheba. In Job 31:1, Job made a covenant with his eyes. In Proverbs 23:7, as a man thinks in his heart, so he is. In Matthew 12:34, you speak out of the abundance of your heart. In 2 Corinthians 10:5, you can take every thought captive. In Psalm 119, we see how we can do this. Read Psalm 119:9-11, and begin memorizing Bible verses. Once memorized, you can meditate on those verses regardless where you are, and regardless when it is.

10. **Be honest**

    It is amazing when someone says: "I'll be honest with you" or "Let me tell you the truth". Do they say that because they usually lie? Being known as an honest person takes time. However, a single lie can destroy an honest reputation. Be honest in all your dealings.

11. **Be observant**

    When you drive, it is called "defensive driving", because you are constantly on guard as the driver. Being observant includes where you are going, the surroundings, what you watch, read, attend, and more. Just by observing people, you will learn a lot. When you observe, you may not even be noticed, and you seldom, if ever, need to talk! As I say: Be alert. The world needs more lerts.

12. **Keep your mind and body clean**

    The mind: Everything you do or say will have its origin in your mind. It may be in an instant, with an emergency decision, followed by an action. It might simmer in your mind before you decide. Regardless, your speech and action come from within you first. It is imperative for you to guard what you see and think. Invisibly put a funnel over your head, and stop any thought before that thought might cause you trouble. That will help keep your mind clear. Look at Philippians 4:4-10.

    The body: "Personal hygiene" has numerous aspects, including, but not limited to clothes, teeth, cleanliness, how you smell, appear, and more. Remember the saying is: "you only get one chance at a good first impression". Right or wrong; good or bad; people will form their "first impression" of you BEFORE you say a word. The way you take care of yourself, and present yourself, really do speak loudly about YOU.

13. **Enjoy life**

    Some people are quiet. Some are talkers. Some people love to read. Some enjoy a park, or riding a bicycle. Some people enjoy television. Some prefer working with their hands. There is no "single-way" to do it, but enjoy life with what makes you happy. Do not self-judge yourself. Do not dwell on your past. Instead, enjoy your family and friends day-by-day.

14. Be kind

The Golden Rule really is awesome, and it is taken from Matthew 7:12. People talk about a "random act of kindness". That is usually something quick, almost insignificant, regarding a stranger. That is great. Summarize it this way: just be nice (kind) to everyone, all the time. Say thank you. Show appreciation. Show common courtesy and respect. Your kindness is most certainly contagious.

15. Take school subjects seriously

I wish someone had yelled that in my ears 65 years ago. There is no do-over, and no belated mercy. Now is the time to take school seriously. Do your homework. Finish your assignments. Be an attentive student. Sit in the front of the class. There are fewer distractions. By doing the hard work now, the rewards will be seen later.

16. Work your job as if you are the owner

That really is wise counsel. No one wants the company to succeed more than the owner. When an employee has that mindset, the owner will most certainly take note. So few employees have good work ethics. However, this type of employee effort is even more rare. There will be unusually excellent results and rewards when you work AS IF you are the owner. Trust me on this.

17. Discern truth

This may be a bit tricky. To "discern" means to know without factual evidence. So, to discern truth, you must be familiar with truth. Most bank employees can stop a counterfeit bill because they handle real money all the time. TRUTH begins in the Bible, with Biblical principles. The more TRUTH you know, the easier it will be for you to discern truth. Be cautious and suspicious, especially in your dealings with strangers, and ANYTHING coming to you via computer. Colossians 2:1-3 says all the treasures of wisdom and knowledge are hidden in Jesus.

18. **Respect others**

    We extend a certain amount of respect to total strangers when we meet them. From that first moment, respect will be built, deepened, or proven wrong, based on experience. President Reagan said, "Trust, but verify". I encourage you to respect others without openly setting yourself up for being treated improperly. You will learn who you can trust, and how much you can honestly trust individuals. Just be cautious as you trust. Even as you learn to trust, be on your guard.

19. **Eat healthy**

    I had two friends. One wore a shirt that said: "I am not overweight. I am just 6 inches too short". The other man would say: "If I had known I would live this long, I would have taken better care of myself". In your life, put healthy food into your body. As an aside, I encourage you to avoid, or stop any harmful habits. Both drugs and cigarettes are known to be life-ending habits. Never start. If you have, QUIT today. My dad smoked from age 11-50. At age 87, he was diagnosed with lung cancer, and gone within two months. Eat healthy.

20. Be true to yourself

There is absolutely nothing in life worth betraying your personal foundation: guard your name and reputation. When all the fluff is blown away, your name and reputation will be enough to keep you going. Let others get to know the real you: anchored in the Bible.

21. Set goals, and work hard

Set realistic, attainable goals, but SET THEM! When you set a goal, determine an exact plan to reach that goal. Sales is an excellent example. Suppose you need to talk to 10 people before one is interested. Suppose you must talk to five interested people to have a single buyer. Then, suppose you want to make five sales in one week. Easy goal: for five sales, I need to make 25 presentations. To make 25 presentations, I need to contact 250 people. Therefore, I can set a realistic goal of talking to 250 people in one week. Make your goals, and then be a diligent worker toward that goal. The definition of insanity is the person who does the same thing, while expecting different results.

22. Find trustworthy friends

Almost everyone has "friends". There is only one way to have trustworthy friends: they must be proven by testing. That trust is built over a period of time and fellowship. Always be cautious, and almost never extend unusual personal information to strangers. Trust will be built over years of friendship. One word of caution. That same trust can be lost with a single betrayal. While you want trustworthy friends, you set the pace by being that trustworthy friend to others.

23. **Talk and listen to old people**

You will never know the depth of those words of wisdom until you are old. I have heard 17 year old teenagers, with two years of driving experience, say: "I've been driving a long time. I know how to text and email while I drive". NOT TRUE. Older drivers can tell you true stories. Old people have DECADES of life experience. Get to know them. As a youth pastor in 1977 and 1978, I took our youth group to nursing homes to visit older people. EVERYONE LOVED IT: patients, youth, and staff.

24. **Study and learn history**

Wallbuilders, in Aledo, Texas, does not obtain original historical documents written since around 1825. They do have close to 80,000 original documents written prior to 1825!! History is now being revised by slanted journalists with an agenda to destroy America from the roots. I will give you three excellent places to start. First, David Barton and Wallbuilders. Next, William Federer, and his expanded ministry: Truth and Liberty Coalition; The American-Minute; and his book, America's God and Country. That one book has 700 pages of quotes, with his bibliography making the book well over 800 pages. He has thoroughly documented his sources. There is another fabulous book, written by Benjamin F. Morris. He worked in the U.S. Capitol, and spent over 10 years doing research for his book inside the Library of Congress, between 1840-1860. His book is entitled: The Christian Life and Character of the Civil Institution of the United States; and the text is 1,059 pages. You must know American history from factual history!

25. Help others

That is easy to understand, but not easy to do. Most people are lazy, selfish, and unavailable to help. True, you will get taken advantage of, when you help others, but it is the right thing to do. Make yourself a servant to others, and you will always have friends... who will "need" you. Helping others really is fun.

26. Respect your parents

Admittedly, many children do not grow up with both biological parents by their side daily, in the same house. Your generation can change that dynamic as you trust me in this book, and commit to living out the Golden Rule (Matthew 7:12 and Matthew 22:34-40). Remember, you are the first generation of your legacy. Respect your parents. Give them first-time obedience. Be attentive to their counsel. Trust their decisions as you grow up. Someday, you will be a parent, and you will appreciate your children respecting you. Years ago, my two brothers and I had a conversation, with 100% agreement. At the time of our conversation, Tom was about 68 years old, I was about 66, and Robert about 55 years old. Mom was 90 years old, and Dad had been gone about five years. That makes the year of our discussion about 2012. We unanimously agreed, at our respective ages, NONE of us had ever disrespected Mom or Dad; we had NEVER told them "No, I will not do what you tell me to do"; and we had NEVER used profanity in either Mom or Dad's presence. When Mom died at age 98, Robert and I confirmed that again: NEVER!! I encourage you to respect your parents.

27. Respect your teachers

Your teacher (in public school) is a college graduate, trained to teach young children. They have almost consistently given up a high income career to be able to teach you. Show them respect. Be attentive. Ask questions. Do not cause trouble. Do your homework. Be an example for other students. Show appreciation and respect verbally as well in class itself. ONE MORE. For my family members who are educated at home, you BETTER respect your teacher!! She most likely gave birth to you.

28. Be polite

There is absolutely NOTHING WRONG with being polite. Open doors for other people. Say yes ma'am; yes sir; no ma'am; no sir. Say thank you. Live out the Golden Rule. Just be polite.

29. Exercise

We constantly hear doctors say: eat properly, and exercise. There are countless ways to exercise. Join a gym. Walk. Ride a bicycle. Do calisthenics at home. Do not push yourself to injury. Just do a slow, steady exercise. That will help keep your weight and your heart going properly. Be consistent. Many years ago, I read a story about a woman about 55 years old, who started jogging. She jogged less than a half-block on her first run. In less than two years, she ran a half-marathon (13.1). Start exercising!

30. Never give up

I saw an interesting drawing years ago. A pelican had a frog in its mouth, and almost nothing but the four legs was visible. The back legs appeared to be kicking, and the front legs were visibly choking the pelican. The caption beneath said: "Never give up". There is a familiar saying: "Quitters never win, and winners never quit". When I went to Navy Diver's School in August, 1968, we started with about 135 students. As I remember, 27 graduated. I cannot remember how many times I wanted to quit, but it was NUMEROUS times. However, I have the certificate showing I graduated, and at age 76 now (2022), I can proudly say I was a Navy Frogman!! Maybe you will need to slow down, or change plans, but never quit. You will always regret quitting. May that decision never be on your internal barometer!!

31. You are a child now. Someday you will be a parent with children.

One vital responsibility of a parent is to prepare each child to properly assume their role in society as an adult. That one issue has NUMEROUS individual aspects. As a child yourself, you are most likely oblivious to the intricacies of adult life, and decisions that follow you through life. My counsel to you TODAY, is this: Trust your parents. Listen to them. Give them respect. Give them your attention. Give them "first time obedience", and give them no argument, back-talking, or disrespect. As a child yourself, think this way: if you were the parent, and your child did exactly what you want to do now, would you be happy or upset? Then, make the right decision NOW. You really only get one chance at being a child. The decisions you make today will follow you as an adult and parent. Proverbs 20:11 is a solid verse to know.

32. How do you want to be remembered?

Most people spend zero time with this question until they are retired. Even then, many people have no regard as to HOW people will remember them. I encourage you, here and now, sit down and think: how do you want to be remembered. People **WILL** remember you: good, bad, or indifferent. The "HOW" of you being remembered will depend on how you conduct yourself each day, with each individual. I will give you an innocent illustration that, for me, is a life time treasure. At age 10, I had a life-long, memorable conversation with Joe DiMaggio. He probably forgot the conversation before the sun went down that very day, but I remember virtually every detail, almost 70 years later. Joe was signing autographs, with at least 50 of us kids standing close by. From behind, I was almost crushed up against the rail by Mr. DiMaggio. He said to me "Kid, are you okay?" I said "Yes Sir", and my 8x10 photo of him was signed quickly. You **WILL** be remembered. You decide HOW, by how you live day-by-day.

33. **You can make a difference!** One person can do that. Lannie Mae made a difference in my life when I was five years old. Walter made a difference in my life when I was seven years old. Kenneth Lee and his family made a difference in my life when I was 18. Lannie Mae was the Black babysitter for Tom and me in 1950. Walter was our Black mailman in 1951. Kenneth and his parents were the Black family I lived with for almost two month in Washington, D.C. in 1965. Those, and other "unknowns" helped mold me into who I am today. Again, you **WILL** be remembered. Make those memories good.

LAY THE FOUNDATION

A family is only as strong as the foundation, so we will start with a FEW passages in a chronological order (almost).

I encourage you to start with Malachi 4:6, the very last verse in the Old Testament.

1-2. Exodus 12;26, 27
-Verse 26 – Children will ask about the Passover
-Verse 27 – Parents will explain the purpose of Passover

3. Deuteronomy 4:9, 10

        -Verse 9 – Take heed; be diligent; lest you forget and depart
        -Verse 9 – Teach to your sons, and thy sons' sons
        -Verse 10 – God has told you to teach your children

4. Deuteronomy 6:4-9
        -Verse 6 – This is a command
        -Verse 7 – Teach diligently to your children
        -Verse 7 – Teach while you sit, walk, lay down, rise up
        -Verse 8 – Bind your teaching so it is visible
        -Verse 9 – Write on your house and gates: visible

5. Deuteronomy 6:20-25
        -Verse 20 – Your children will ask about testimonies, statutes, judgments
        -Verse 21-24 – Explain the protection and provision of God
        -Verse 25 – We should observe to do all He commands

6. Deuteronomy 11:18, 19
        -Verse 18 – Lay these treasures in your heart
        -Verse 19 – Teach them to your children as Deuteronomy 6:7 says

7. Deuteronomy 32:45-47
        -Verse 45 – Moses to all of Israel
        -Verse 46 – Set your hearts to all I say to you today
        -Verse 46 – Command your children to do all I say
        -Verse 47 – This is your life, and this will prolong your days

8. Psalm 22:30, 31
   -Verse 30 – A seed; a generation to serve the Lord
   -Verse 31 – Declare His righteousness to the next generation

9. Psalm 44:1 – Our fathers have told us what works You have done, O Lord

10. Psalm 48:12-14
    -Verse 13 – Tell it to the generation to come
    -Verse 14 – This God is our God; He will guide your life

11. Psalm 78:4
    -Verse 4 – We will not hide them from our children
    -Verse 4 – Show the coming generation His praises; strengths; works

12. Psalm 89:4 (God speaking)
    -Verse 4 – Thy seed I will establish forever
    -Verse 4 – I will build thy throne to all generations

13. Psalm 102:18 – Write for the generation to come, people are created to praise Him

14. Psalm 102:28 – The seed of the children of your servants will be established before you

15. Isaiah 38:19
    -Verse 19 – The living, the living, shall praise You O Lord

-Verse 19 – The father shall make known Your truth to his children

16. Psalm 145:4 – One generation shall praise Thy works to another, and shall declare Thy mighty works

To my beloved family: biological, blended, and spiritual; these 16 passages are not even the tip of the spiritual iceberg of Biblical truth: the family has been designed by the Lord to be the primary facility to teach and prepare the next generation. That process is to start today, with you. Always, **ALWAYS KNOW**: You are the first generation of your legacy.

This has been just the beginning. We will now almost exclusively examine what Proverbs says about the family. As you know, Proverbs is considered one of "The Wisdom Books". May the Lord implant His wisdom into your heart regarding your family, and your legacy.

GENERIC THOUGHTS: WE CONCENTRATE ON INSTRUCTION

Cars have an owner's manual. Products have an instruction sheet for assembly. A teacher has the class curriculum for instruction. The family provides instruction for daily life. From Proverbs, let's consider some generic thoughts.

- ✓ Verse 1:2 – We are to know instruction
- ✓ Verse 1:3 – We are to receive the instruction of wisdom

- ✓ Verse 1:7 – Fools despise instruction
- ✓ Verse 1:8 – The child is to hear the instruction of the Dad
- ✓ Verse 4:1 – Young children, hear the instruction of your Dad
- ✓ Verse 4:13 – Take fast hold of instruction, and do not let go of it
- ✓ Verse 5:12 – Do not hate instruction
- ✓ Verse 5:23 – You will die without instruction
- ✓ Verse 8:10 – Receive instruction, not silver
- ✓ Verse 8:33 – Hear instructions, and be wise. Do not refuse instruction
- ✓ Verse 9:9 – Give instruction to a wise man, and he will be wiser
- ✓ Verse 10:17 – Keep instruction
- ✓ Verse 12:1 – Whoever loves instruction loves knowledge
- ✓ Verse 13:1 – A wise son hears his father's instruction
- ✓ Verse 13:18 – Poverty and shame to him who refuses instruction
- ✓ Verse 15:5 – A fool despises his Dad's instruction
- ✓ Verse 15:32 – Whoever refuses instruction despises his own soul
- ✓ Verse 15:33 – The fear of the Lord is the instruction of wisdom
- ✓ Verse 16:22 – The instruction of fools is folly
- ✓ Verse 19:20 – Receive instruction to be wise
- ✓ Verse 19:27 – Quit hearing instruction that causes you to err
- ✓ Verse 23:12 – Apply your heart to instruction
- ✓ Verse 23:23 – Buy instruction, and do not sell it
- ✓ Verse 24:32 – Receive instruction

SAY – DO – ATTITUDE: INTRODUCTION FOR THIS SECTION

Proverbs is 31 chapters, with 915 verses, covering virtually every aspect of life. The middle chapters, 10-15, are unusual. Those chapters have 184 verses. Within those six chapters, and 184 verses, are approximately 140 repetitive uses of the exact same word: "but". The word "but" in these chapters shows a contrast between two almost opposing views. For this section of the book, I am using the "good news" contrast. You decide if you want to review the opposite. One illustration, selected 100% randomly, is this: Proverbs 11:13 "He who goes about as a talebearer reveals secrets, BUT he who is trustworthy conceals a matter".

As you look at the following list, you could analyze it in at least three categories: what you say; what you do; and your attitude (character). I can tell you this with certainty: the more you study these, the more Proverbs becomes yours. For me, I spent two years, virtually every day, looking at these 915 verses, and the conclusion was eight study books with eight different topics, and well over 500 lessons!!

Proverbs Chapter 10 (by verse)
1- A wise son makes a glad father
2- The righteous delivers from death
3- The Lord will not allow the righteous to hunger
4- The hand of the diligent makes rich
5- He who gathers in the summer is a son who acts wisely
6- Blessings are on the head of the righteous

7- The memory of the righteous is blessed
8- The wise of heart will receive commands
9- He who walks in integrity walks securely
11- The mouth of the righteous is a fountain of life
12- Love covers all transgressions
13- Wisdom is found on the lips of the discerning
14- Wise men store up knowledge
17- He who keeps instruction is on the path of life
19- He who restrains his lips is wise
21- The lips of the righteous feed many
25- The righteous is an everlasting foundation
27- The fear of the Lord prolongs life
28- The hope of the righteous is gladness
29- The way of the Lord is a stronghold to the upright
30- The righteous will never be shaken
31- The mouth of the righteous flows with wisdom
32- The lips of the righteous bring forth what is acceptable

Proverbs Chapter 11
1- A just weight is a delight to the Lord
2- With the humble there is wisdom
3- The integrity of the upright will guide them
4- Righteousness delivers from death
5- The righteousness of the blameless will smooth his way
6- The righteousness of the upright will deliver them
8- The righteous is delivered from trouble
9- Through knowledge the righteous will be delivered
11- By the blessing of the upright a city is exalted
12- A man of understanding keeps silent
13- He who is faithful and trustworthy conceals a matter

14- In an abundance of counselors there is safety
17- The merciful man does himself good
18- He who sows righteousness gets a true reward
20- The blameless in their walk are the Lord's delight
21- The descendants of the righteous will be delivered
23- The desire of the righteous is only good
27- He who diligently seeks good finds favor
28- The righteous will flourish like the green leaf
30- The fruit of the righteous is a tree of life

Proverbs Chapter 12
1- Whoever loves instruction loves knowledge
2- A good man will obtain favor from the Lord
3- The root of the righteous will not be moved
4- An excellent wife is the crown of her husband
5- The thoughts of the righteous are just
6- The mouth of the upright will deliver them
7- The house of the righteous will stand
8- A man will be praised according to his insight and wisdom
10- A righteous man has regard for the lives of animals
11- He who tills his land will have plenty of bread
12- The root of the righteous yields fruit
13- The righteous will escape from trouble
15- A man who listens to counsel is wise
16- A prudent man conceals dishonor
17- He who speaks truth tells what is righteous
18- The tongue of the wise brings healing and health
19- Truthful lips will be established forever
20- Counselors of peace have joy
21- No harm befalls the righteous (just)
22- Those who deal faithfully are His delight
23- A prudent man conceals knowledge

24- The hand of the diligent will rule
25- A good word makes the heart glad
26- The righteous is a guide to his neighbor
27- The precious possession of a man is his diligence
28- The way of righteousness is life, with no death

Proverbs Chapter 13

1- A wise son accepts his Dad's discipline
2- From the fruit of his mouth a man enjoys good
4- The soul of the diligent is made fat
6- Righteousness guards the blameless in life
9- The light of the righteous rejoices
10- Wisdom is with those who receive counsel
11- The one who gathers by labor increases it
12- Desire fulfilled is a tree of life
13- The one who fears the commandment will be rewarded
15- Good understanding produces favor
16- Every prudent man acts with knowledge
17- A faithful envoy (ambassador) brings healing
18- He who regards reproof will be honored
20- He who walks with wise men will be wise
21- The righteous will be rewarded with prosperity

Proverbs Chapter 14

1- The wise woman builds her house
2- He who walks in his uprightness fears the Lord
3- The lips of the wise will preserve them
5- A faithful witness will not lie
8- The wisdom of the prudent is to understand his way
9- Among the upright there is good will
11- The tent of the upright will flourish

14- A good man will be satisfied in his heart
15- A prudent man will consider his ways
16- A wise man is cautious
16- A wise man turns away from evil
18- The prudent are crowned with knowledge
21- Happy is he who is gracious to the poor
22- Mercy and truth will be to those who devise good
23- In all labor there is profit
25- A truthful witness saves lives
29- He who is slow to anger has great understanding
30- A tranquil heart is life to the body
31- He who honors the Lord is gracious to the needy
32- The righteous has a refuge when he dies
33- Wisdom rests in the heart of him with understanding
34- Righteousness exalts a nation

Proverbs Chapter 15
1- A gentle answer turns away wrath
2- The tongue of the wise makes knowledge acceptable
4- A soothing (wholesome) tongue is a tree of life
5- He who regards reproof is prudent
7- The lips of the wise spread knowledge
8- The prayer of the upright is the Lord's delight
9- The Lord loves him who pursues righteousness
13- A joyful heart makes a cheerful face
18- Being slow to anger pacifies contentions
19- The path of the upright is made plain
20- A wise son makes a Dad glad
21- A man of understanding walks straight
22- With many counselors plans are established
26- The words of the pure are pleasant

27- He who hates bribes will live
28- The heart of the wise ponders how to answer
29- The Lord hears the prayers of the righteous
32- He who listens to reproof acquires an understanding heart
33- The fear of the Lord is the instruction for wisdom
33- Before honor comes humility

Here is a simple (but not quick) optional assignment. Using the above verses from Proverbs 10-15, make as many different lists as you can. Then, taking one list at a time, develop life principles for yourself, your family, and your ministry. To help you get started, here is a list of possible options for your lists:

- Attitude
- What you say
- Consequences
- Wicked
- Good
- The Lord
- Family
- Righteous
- What you do
- Heart
- Result
- Bad

Be creative and have fun. There is great joy in your in-depth, individual Bible study. Dig deep. The rewards are eternal.

CONCLUSION

The entire premise of this Christmas gift is clear. Your 76 year old Dad, Paw Paw, is giving you a variety of solid life principles for you, my family. You decide how you want to use and apply these. However, there is one absolute certainty. Each of us, including me, are currently responsible to live based on these principles; and at a time - certain future moment, we will individually give an accountant to the Lord Jesus for how we applied these principles to our lives.

You know I am as available as possible to help you.

I love you,
Paw Paw

INTERESTING INSTRUCTIONS FROM DAD

Even when I was 60 years old, and my Dad was 87, when he told me to do something, my instant response was "Yes sir". I did not question him. To me, at age 60, with grandchildren of my own, I did what my Dad said, when he said it, without any debate or argument. My brothers did that, too. Proverbs has a few instructions for children from their Dad.

- Verse 23:19 – Hear me, my son
- Verse 23:19 – Be wise, my son
- Verse 23:19 – My son, guide your heart in the right way

- Verse 23:20 – My son, do not be a heavy drinker
- Verse 23:21 – My son, do not be a glutton
- Verse 23:22 – My son, listen to me
- Verse 23:22 – Do not despise your Mom when she is old
- Verse 23:23 – Buy the truth, and do not sell it
- Verse 23:23 – Buy wisdom, instruction, and understanding
- Verse 23:24 – You are a wise, righteous child, and I rejoice
- Verse 23:26 – My son, give me your heart
- Verse 23:26 – My son, learn my ways
- Verse 24:14 – My son, the knowledge of wisdom is good for your soul
- Verse 24:14 – When you find wisdom, there is a reward
- Verse 24:21 – My son, fear the Lord

There are more generic instructions for you as a child, or parent with children

- Verse 28:7 – Whoever keeps the law is a wise son
- Verse 28:7 – A companion of rioters shames his Dad
- Verse 28:24 – Do not steal from your Mom or Dad
- Verse 29:3 – Whoever loves wisdom rejoices your Dad

Proverbs uses the word "generation", and those verses add insight to a child, the parents, and the family itself: "This Generation":

- Verse 30:11 – Curses their father
- Verse 30:11 – Does not bless their Mom
- Verse 30:12 – Is pure in their own eyes
- Verse 30:12 – Is not washed from their filthiness
- Verse 30:14 – Has teeth like swords

- Verse 30:14 – Devours the poor and needy
- Verse 30:17 – Mocks their Dad, and despises their Mom

My Beloved Family, may WE be the example for others!

I love you,

Paw Paw

DAD GETS HIS INSTRUCTION

Dad is responsible for instructing the family. But from where does Dad get that instruction? Excellent question.
- Proverbs 4:1 – The child is to know understanding
- Proverbs 4:2 – Each child must not ignore his Dad's law
- Proverbs 4:2 – Good doctrine is the spiritual meat provided by Dad to the child
- Proverbs 4:3 – There was a time Dad was the child himself
- Proverbs 4:4 – This is where the rubber meets the road. Your Dad is to have received instruction from his Dad, so he will know how to instruct his own children.
- Proverbs 4:4 – The child is to retain his Dad's word in his heart, and keep the commandments of his Dad.
-

There may well be times when a child grows up without the spiritual instruction of his Dad. Two points. Some adult should help that child learn spiritual truths as he ages. Second, that child will become a teenager and adult. He is ultimately responsible for his own spiritual maturity. But Dad, the primary responsibility is in your hands.

There is one more key point to this text (Proverbs 4:1-4). Solomon (the Dad) was teaching spiritual truth to his son; and Solomon proudly told his son he had received that instruction from his own Dad, David. That is three generations: David, Solomon, and the grandson. That, **Beloved Family**, is the multi-generational faithfulness principle.

As I have said so often, you are the first generation of your legacy.
I love you,

Paw Paw

Proverbs 4 is such a rich chapter for the family. Let's keep these principles going in our family.

In verse 4:5, we are to get wisdom, get understanding, do not forget either, and trust what your Dad says.

In verse 4:6, love wisdom, and do not forsake wisdom. Wisdom will preserve and keep you.

Proverbs 4:3-12: Solomon
Verse 3 – Solomon was a son, loved by his Dad
Verse 4 – Solomon remembered what his Dad taught him
Verse 10 – Solomon was confident in his own instruction

Verse 11 – Solomon taught what his Dad taught
Verse 12 – As they say: "Been there, done that"
Proverbs 4:1-20: Dad is responsible for:
Verse 1 – Instruction
Verse 2 – Good doctrine
Verse 10 – Sayings
Verse 11 – Teach the way of wisdom
Verse 11 – Lead the child in the right path
Verse 20 – Speak things of VALUE to your child
Proverbs 4:23-27 – Dad gives clear instruction
Verse 23 – Keep your heart with all diligence
Verse 23 – The issues of life start in the heart
Verse 24 – A child should put away perverse words and eyes
Verse 25 – As Job, put a guard around your eyes (Job 31:1)
Verse 26 – Let all your ways be established – ponder the path of your feet
Verse 27 – Remove your feet from evil
Proverbs 4 would be a classic chapter for you to do more independent study.

INSTRUCTIONS FROM DAD

In this brief section, we will look at a few simple instructions from Dad, from within Proverbs.
Proverbs 1:8, 9
Children are to hear the instruction of Dad. Verse 9 says that instruction will be an ornament of grace on your head, and chains on your neck. As beautiful as that sounds, instruction makes you a priceless treasure.

Proverbs 4:1, 2

Dad has at least two things to give his children: instruction, and good doctrine. Each child should seek understanding, without forsaking his Dad's law.

Proverbs 8:10, 11

Dad's instruction is more than valuable. It is to be sought over silver; and knowledge is more valuable than gold. Wisdom is better than rubies, and there is no comparison to instruction, knowledge, and wisdom.

Proverbs 13:1

A son who hears his Dad's instruction is considered wise.

Proverbs 15:5

A son who despises his Dad's instruction is a fool.

Proverbs 19:27

This is a word of caution. Each child should stop, and refrain from listening to bad instruction that causes you to stray from truth and knowledge. That may come from peer pressure.

WHAT DAD SHOULD PROVIDE

The father is the key ingredient for a successful family. True, this book is written by Paw Paw to my family for Christmas 2022. Also true, I know that not all of you have had daily access, instruction, encouragement, and love from your biological Dad. I know that! What your Dad did or did not do is **NOT** your responsibility. How you respond is on you. Here is my encouragement to you as we begin to study the family as described in Proverbs.

If your Dad was faithful, loving, and encouraging, let him know how much you love, appreciate, and respect him. If he was not, you still need to love him, and work to build some type of relationship. If he is no longer with us, treasure the good memories you have. Now to you. As you age and become an adult, it is your responsibility to set the spiritual standards, and the spiritual example to your family: biological, blended, and spiritual. From this moment, the following instructions are for you personally, from the Lord, in the inerrant Book of Proverbs: male or female; child or adult; husband or wife; Mother or Dad. These instructions are for YOU. Allow me to be very specific, with the three newest family members. My great-grandson, Finn, was born May 7, 2021. My great-granddaughter, Hattie Brave, was born on August 14, 2021. My Great-grandson, Henry, is scheduled to arrive before Christmas of this year. Aside: this was edited on December 1, 2022, the day AFTER Henry was born. Welcome to the family, Big Guy! You three are the youngest, unable to care for yourself. You will grow up: a child, youth, teenager, adult, husband, wife, Mom, Dad, GRANDPARENT and GREAT-GRANDPARENT. At some stage in life, these principles will be for you. This book is me, Paw Paw, giving encouraging words to YOU, before I breathe my final breath. With everything inside me, I implore you to live for Jesus, and instill Biblical principles into your life, and all the lives around you.

One more serious thought. To each individual who reads this book, my desire is to encourage you in life. I will always encourage you. However, there is a Biblical standard for our lives, and this book is my attempt to give you wisdom to live by, in every phase of life! Admittedly, each of us is both **responsible** for our decisions, actions, and words; and we will be **accountable** to the Lord for those decisions, actions, and words. May each reader commit to a life pleasing to the Lord. Now, let's start with Dad.

We will start with a spiritual warm-up. In Proverbs, let's begin with a single word admonition for the Dad, to use in the family.

>Wisdom: 1:1-3; 1:5; 5:1
>Words: 2:1; 4:4; 4:20; 7:1
>Commandments: 2:1; 3:1; 4:4; 6:20; 7:1; 7:2
>Instruction: 4:1; 8:10
>Doctrine: 4:2
>Law: 3:1; 4:2; 7:2
>Sayings: 4:10; 4:20
>In Proverbs 23:26 "Let thine eyes observe my ways"

We are just in the spiritual warm-up. Of course there is more.

I love you, Family!
Paw Paw

THE VIRTUOUS WOMAN

Proverbs 31:10 talks about the virtuous woman. In 22 verses (verses 10-31), there are 41 great traits of a virtuous woman. By the way, I am guessing that virtuous woman was well on her way to those traits as a young girl, because of her family setting. To my grand-daughters, you can be that virtuous woman.

I love you,
Paw Paw

Verse 31:10 – Her worth is far above rubies
Verse 31:11 – The heart of her husband trusts her
Verse 31:11 – Her husband has no need of spoil
Verse 31:12 – She does him good, and not evil, all her life
Verse 31:13 – She works willingly with her hands
Verse 31:14 – She is like a merchant's ship
Verse 31:14 – She brings food for her family
Verse 31:15 – She gets up when it is still dark
Verse 31:15 – She gives meat to her family
Verse 31:15 – She gives a portion of meat to others
Verse 31:16 – She considers a field, and buys it
Verse 31:16 – With the fruit of her hands, she plants a vineyard
Verse 31:17 – She is a strong woman
Verse 31:17 – She strengthens her arms
Verse 31:18 – She knows her merchandise is good
Verse 31:18 – Her light does not go out at night
Verse 31:19 – She works diligently
Verse 31:19 – She has excellent work ethics
Verse 31:20 – She helps the poor
Verse 31:20 – She reaches out to the needy
Verse 31:21 – She is not afraid of the snow
Verse 31:21 – She makes clothes for her family
Verse 31:22 – She is a creative designer
Verse 31:22 – She dresses nicely
Verse 31:23 – Her husband is known in the gates
Verse 31:24 – She makes linen and sells it
Verse 31:24 – She delivers to others
Verse 31:25 – Strength and honor are her clothing
Verse 31:25 – She will rejoice in the future
Verse 31:26 – She speaks with wisdom
Verse 31:26 – She is conscientious, using the law of kindness
Verse 31:27 – She is not lazy

Verse 31:28 – Her children bless her
Verse 31:28 – Her husband praises her
Verse 31:29 – She excels all virtuous woman
Verse 31:30 – Favor is deceitful
Verse 31:30 – Beauty is vain
Verse 31:30 – She is praised because she fears the Lord
Verse 31:31 – Give her the fruit of her hands
Verse 31:31 – Let her works praise her in the gates

To my beloved family, all of our children need a virtuous Mom, and I am blessed to have a family full of them.

I love you,
Paw Paw

WHAT THE MOM SHOULD PROVIDE

As we did with Dad, we will start with a brief spiritual warm up. From Proverbs, let's get a glimpse of the ministry of the Mother, using a few words per verse.

Verse 1:8 – Law 6:20
Verse 4:3 – (Love)
Verse 19:26 – (Patience) – Do not chase her away
Verse 20:20 – Do not curse your Mom
Verse 23:22 – Do not despise her when she is old
Verse 23:25 – Be glad and rejoice
Verse 28:24 – Rob from your Mom, and you are a companion to a destroyer
Verse 29:15 – A child left to himself brings shame to his Mom
Verse 30:11 – There is a generation that does not bless their Mom

Verse 30:17 – Ravens and young eagles will pick out your eyes if you refuse to obey your Mom
Verse 31:1 – Mom, teach your children

Yes, I realize some of the above are for children, and those verses were intentionally included. Your Mom must hold a special place in your heart, your daily life, and in your family.

AN INTRODUCTION FOR CHILDREN

Proverbs speaks boldly to and about children. Again, we start with a spiritual warm-up view of children.

Verse 4:1 – Each child should hear the instruction of Dad
Verse 4:1 – Each child should attend to know understanding
Verse 5:7 – Do not depart from the words of your Dad
Verse 7:24 – Hearken to your Dad, and attend to his words
Verse 8:32 – Keep the ways of your Dad
Verse 20:7 – Children are blessed when Dad walks in integrity
Verse 31:28 – Children should rise up and bless your Mom

The mother has a special place of honor, dignity, respect, appreciation, and love within your family. Dads, make that a reality. Children, make that your daily habit. May all who know you, be able to brag about the way you treat your Mom.

We have done the warm-up, and we need to get started on the child/children. Let's begin with a few specific comments about children from the Book of Wisdom - Proverbs.

Verse 20:11 – A child is known by his doings (works)
Verse 20:11 – A child is known by whether his works are pure and right
Verse 22:6 – Trained properly, the child will not depart from that teaching when he becomes an adult himself
Verse 23:13 – Correction is not bad for a child
Verse 23:24 – The Dad of a wise child will greatly rejoice

Verse 29:15 – When left on his own, a child brings his Mother to shame

As you can see, solid spiritual instruction is vital to a child as he grows up. Mom and Dad, that is your spiritual responsibility.

INSTRUCTIONS FOR CHILDREN

We have arrived at the "meat" of this book. This book is my Christmas, 2022 gift to my family: biological, blended, and spiritual. To those related to me by blood, I am now THE PATRIARCH; the oldest; the senior family member. At age 76, some say I should not buy food with an expiration date farther than this weekend. Perhaps. But then, none of us have any guarantee we will see the sunrise tomorrow. This book is designed and intended to be my parting words, to my family, while I am still living.

In August 2012, I started a two year project. The result was eight different studies, with well over 500 different lessons, from within the 31 chapters and 915 verses in Proverbs. One of those studies was on Proverbs and the Family. The following instructions were gleaned by me, from the Book of Proverbs. I need to be thorough here since this book most likely will not have a "second edition". Consider Proverbs, the family, and YOU: training, instructions, and principles for children (and adults).

Verse 1:4 – The need is for knowledge and discretion
Verse 1:8 – Children should hear instruction from your Dad
Verse 1:8 – Children should not forsake Mom's Law
Verse 1:10 – Children should not yield to enticement and peer pressure

Verse 2:1 – Receive the words and instruction of your Dad
Verse 2:1 – Hide Dad's commandments within you
Verse 2:2 – Incline your ear to wisdom
Verse 2:2 – Apply your heart to understanding
Verse 2:3 – Cry out for knowledge
Verse 2:3 – Lift up your voice for understanding
Verse 2:4 – Search for wisdom as if it was a hidden treasure
Verse 2:11 – Discretion will follow those who apply wisdom
Verse 2:11 – Understanding will keep you
Verse 2:12 – Wisdom will deliver you from the way of evil people
Verse 3:1 – Do not forget the law of your Dad
Verse 3:1 – Keep the commandments of your Dad
Verse 3:3 – Keep mercy and truth
Verse 3:5 – Trust the Lord with all your heart
Verse 3:5 – Do not lean on your own understanding
Verse 3:6 – In all your ways, acknowledge Him
Verse 3:9 – Honor the Lord with your first-fruit in life
Verse 3:11 – Do not grow weary when the Lord chastens you
Verse 3:21 – Keep wisdom
Verse 3:21 – Keep discretion
Verse 3:25 – Do not be afraid of sudden fear
Verse 3:27 – Do not withhold good to whom it is due
Verse 3:29 – Do not plan evil against your neighbor-friend
Verse 3:31 – Do not envy bad people
Verse 4:1 – Listen to the instruction of your Dad
Verse 4:4 – Keep his instruction in your heart
Verse 4:5 – get wisdom, understanding, and do not forsake either
Verse 4:13 – Hold on to your Dad's instruction
Verse 4:14 – Do not go with unsavory people
Chapter 4 – The results: 4, 6, 6, 8, 8, 9, 9, 10, 12, 12, 13

Chapter 4 – More instructions: 20, 20, 21, 21, 23, 24, 24, 25, 25, 26, 26, 27, 27, 27

Chapter 4 – More results: 22, 22, 23

Verse 5:1 – Listen to my wisdom and understanding

Verse 5:2 – Be discreet in daily life

Verse 5:7 – Do not depart from what your Dad teaches you

Verse 6:6 – To everyone: study the ant for practical life principles

Verse 6:20 – Keep your Dad's instruction

Verse 6:20 – Do not forsake the law of your Mom

Verse 6:21 – Put their teaching safely in your heart

Verse 7:1 – Keep your Dad's words and commandments

Verse 7:2 – Keep your Dad's law as the apple of your eye

Verse 10:1 – A wise child makes a glad father

Verse 10:5 – A wise child has good work ethics

Verse 13:1 – A wise child listens to Dad's instruction

Verse 17:6 – Grandchildren are the crown of old men

Verse 17:6 – The glory of children is their Dad

Verse 19:13 – A foolish child is calamity to Dad

Verse 19:18 – Chasten the child while there is hope

Verse 19:27 – When a child ignores instruction, he will err from the words of knowledge

Verse 20:11 – A child is known by what he does

Verse 20:20 – Do not curse your Mom or Dad

Verse 22:6 – Properly training a child is productive later

Verse 22:15 – Foolishness is bound in the heart of a child

Verse 23:15 – Parents rejoice over a wise-hearted child

Verse 23:16 – Dad rejoices when his children speak properly

Verse 23:17 – A child should not envy bad people in his heart

Verse 23:17 – A child should fear the Lord every day, all day

I readily admit this is a lengthy list for children, but it was not an exhaustive list from Proverbs. One thing I did leave out was the result of good children. That would be an interesting project: to go back through this list for results in verses close by. GOOD NEWS: Your children are priceless, and worth every moment you pour into them!! To my children, grandchildren, and great-grandchildren:

I love you,
Paw Paw

MORE INSTRUCTION FOR A CHILD

This may be repetitive, but if you have a favorite song, you enjoy it each time. Proverbs is rich for the family, and for children. Each child can honor your Dad with these verses.

Verse 4:1 – Hear the instruction of your Dad
Verse 5:7 – Hear me now
Verse 7:24 – Hearken to me
Verse 7:24 – Attend to my words
Verse 8:32 – Hearken unto me
Verse 13:22; 14:26; 15:11; 17:6; 17:6
Verse 20:7 – For the Dad, his children are blessed
Verse 31:28 – For the Mom, her children bless her
We will now shift gears, and focus on different spiritual meat from Proverbs.
Verse 1:10 – A child should not yield to be enticed
Verse 1:15 – Do not keep company with bad people
Verse 1:15 – Keep away from friendship with bad people
Verse 2:2-5 – A child can understand the fear of the Lord
    -Verse 2 – Incline your ear to wisdom

-Verse 2 – Apply your heart to understanding
-Verse 3 – Search for knowledge
-Verse 4 – Seek wisdom as silver
-Verse 4 – Search for wisdom as a hidden treasure
-Verse 3:11 – A child should not despise the chastening of the Lord
-Verse 3:11 – Do not be weary with the Lord's corrections
-Verse 3:21 – A child should keep sound wisdom and discretion
-Verse 10:5 – Good work ethics are better than laziness
-Verse 19:26 – Do not ignore or rebel against what is taught you by your parents
-Verse 19:27 – Be cautious with peer-pressure
-Verse 22:15 – Foolishness is bound in the heart of a child
-Verse 22:28 – Just thinking: Could these "ancient landmarks" have anything to do with multi-generational faithfulness?
-Verse 23:17 – Do not be envious

The Bible is much more serious than we naturally give it credit.

I love you,
Paw Paw

AS I CONCLUDE

I have chosen the way I want to end this book. As with any display of fireworks, you can almost always count on that final flurry known as "the finale". This is my finale for the family I am now THE SENIOR, bloodline patriarch. True, there are a few relatives older than me, but in the Babington/West bloodline, I am now the patriarch – the old geezer. And yes, I wear that honor with respect, appreciation, and with tremendous responsibility to pass the baton of life to you.

In this section, I am providing more verses from Proverbs for children, Mom, and Dad. I also include encouragement for every individual, regardless of your age. Start the fireworks.

CHILDREN

Verse 1:8 – Hear (listen to) the instruction of your Dad
Verse 1:8 – Do not forsake (ignore) the law of your Mom
Verse 3:11 – Do not despise the chastening of the Lord
Verse 3:11 – Do not grow weary of the Lord's chastening (correction)
Verse 6:20 – Keep your Dad's commandment
Verse 6:20 – Do not forsake/ignore the law of your Mom
Verse 19:13 – A foolish son is the calamity of his Dad
Verse 19:26 – A child who assaults Dad, or drives Mom away
Verse 19:26 – Is a shameful and disgraceful child
Verse 23:15 – When the child's heart is wise, the heart of Dad rejoices
Verse 23:26 – My son give me your heart
Verse 23:26 – My son watch the way I live
Verse 27:11 – My son, be wise, and make my heart glad
MOM
Verse 10:1 – A foolish son is the heaviness of his Mother
Verse 11:16 – A gracious woman retains honor
Verse 12:4 – A virtuous woman is a crown to her husband
Verse 18:22 – Whoever finds a good wife finds a good thing
Verse 18:22 – Whoever finds a good wife obtains favor from the Lord
Verse 19:14 – A prudent wife is from the Lord
Verse 23:24-25 – Your Mom shall rejoice

Verse 29:15 – A child left to himself brings shame to his Mom
Verse 31:10 – A virtuous woman is more valuable than rubies
Verse 31:30 – A woman who fears the Lord shall be praised

It is time for the finale on Dad. In virtually every aspect of life, traced along the way, there is one person who is ultimately responsible. With the United States Military, from E-1 to O-10, each higher rank is more responsible. However, the 0-10 General, with 35 years of military expertise, by protocol, will submit to the new President on his very first day in office. The President of the United States is the Commander-in-Chief of the military: the one person who is responsible. In the family, that is DAD.

DAD IS RESPONSIBLE

Your words
Verse 1:8 – You must have good, solid, Biblical instruction
Verse 1:8 – You must teach Biblical instructions to your children
Verse 2:1 – You must have solid Biblical commandments
Verse 4:2 – You must know Biblical law
Verse 4:11 – Teach, and lead by example
Verse 5:1 – You must apply wisdom and understanding to children
Verse 8:10 – Teach Biblical instruction
Your doctrine
Verse 4:2 – Must be clear, Biblical, life principles, precepts
Verse 4:1-4 – Must be generational, non-changing
Solid spiritual meat for growth
Verse 2:2 – Wisdom and understanding

Verse 3:5 – Trust the Lord daily, in all your ways
Verse 3:9 – Honor the Lord in what you receive
Verse 3:11 – Do not despise when the Lord chastens you, Dad
Verse 4:14 – Teach children to stay away from bad people
Verse 23:17 – Teach them not to envy bad people
Verse 24:21 – Teach them to fear the Lord
What example is Dad
Do as I say
Do as I do
Dad sets the pace, and example to follow
Dad is responsible
This responsibility cannot be delegated or pawned off
Dad, you are responsible
The lack of training a child (22:6) produces:
Verse 19:13 – A foolish child is the calamity of his Dad
Verse 19:26 – A son that causes shame and reproach
Verse 20:20 – A child should not curse Mom or Dad
Verse 28:24 – A child should not steal from Mom or Dad
Verse 30:11 – A generation that does not bless Mom
Verse 30:11 – A generation that curses Dad
Verse 30:17 – They mock their Dad
Verse 30:17 – They despise to obey their Mom
Proper Biblical discipline: **BE VERY CAUTIOUS WHEN YOU APPLY THESE**
Verse 19:18 – Chasten the son while there is hope
Verse 22:15 – The rod of correction
Verse 23:13 – Withhold not correction from the child
Verse 23:14 – Use the rod
Verse 29:15 – The rod and reproof give wisdom
Verse 29:17 – Correct your son

WARNING:

These principles are to encourage and equip your children
These principles are NOT a license for child abuse
Dad should never be a bully, or mean to a child
Everything is to be done to gently guide the child to spiritual maturity
Child abuse is a criminal offense
Dad you are responsible and accountable
The blessings
Verse 10:1 – A wise son makes a proud Dad
Verse 20:7 – His children are blessed
Verse 22:6 – Children will not depart
Verse 23:16 – Dad will rejoice
Verse 23:24 – Dad will have joy from his children
Verse 23:25 – Dad and Mom will both rejoice
Verse 23:25 – Mom will rejoice
Verse 27:11 – Dad's heart will be glad
Dad, you will be remembered
How do you want to be remembered?
Phrase: Like father, like son
How did your Dad teach you?
How do you teach your children?
Verses from Proverbs
-1:8 – My instruction
-3:1 – My law
-5:1 – My wisdom
-7:1 – My words
2. Premise of life
    -Psalm 145:4 – One generation to the next
    -2 Timothy 2:2 – Four generations: Paul, Timothy, faithful men, others
    -Deuteronomy 6:4-9 – Includes solid instructions

3. Food-for-thought for Dad
    -Psalm 127:3-5 – children are a heritage from the Lord
    -Proverbs 22:6 – You are responsible to train them
    -Ephesians 6:4 – In the nurture and admonition of the Lord
    -Psalm 78-1-8 – Teach them to love the Lord
    -Proverbs 22:28 – Do not deviate from Biblical boundaries
    -1 Thessalonians 2:11 – Exhort – comfort – charge them
    -Malachi 4:6 – Mesh your heart with their heart
    -Proverbs 17:6 – Grandchildren are the crown of old men
4. Practical thoughts
    -Your heritage and legacy are remembered by your children
    -You see your future through your children
    -Your values are passed through your children
    -You impact future generations through your children
    -You start multi-generational faithfulness
    -You are the first generation of your legacy
5. It is more than flesh and blood
    -Disciple your blood relatives
    -Disciple your blended family
    -Disciple non-related Christians
    -Encourage everyone
    -Edify everyone close to you
    -Pass the spiritual baton to as many as possible
6. The real blessings of being a Dad
    -"THANK YOU" from those you equip and serve
    -"WELL DONE" from the One Who died for you

7. Final passage: 1 Thessalonians 2:19, 20

This has every appearance that we do, indeed, take something with us to Heaven. It is not property, finances, stature, or possessions. We have the ability to take people with us, and there is NO LIMIT.

Get busy, and know I love you,
Paw Paw

CONCLUSION

The book is yours. You have learned about me, my family, my testimony, and my heart for you. To me, Proverbs 23:26 is an exciting verse. You have read about manners, etiquette, character, family dynamics, genealogy, and legacy. As you lay the book down, you need to be ready to soar spiritually and emotionally. That is your decision. You do not have to do this alone.

Start with OUR FAMILY. Find someone you trust in our family, and be accountable to one another. Dream out loud to each other. Challenge one another in discipleship, prayer, memory verses, and Character Traits. Take the principles in this book, and build spiritual maturity together. Then, branch out.

That is called discipleship. As you start that direction in your life, there is no limit where your legacy will be when you are 76 years old. Your bloodline will be your legacy. Your biological family members will be in your legacy. Your blended family members will be in your legacy. Your spiritual family, by discipleship, will give you numerous great-grandchildren as you intentionally train and disciple others. Therefore, your spiritual family will also be included in your legacy!

With the Church in Thessalonica, Paul spoke of their spiritual legacy in 1 Thessalonians 1:5-10. That, my Beloved Family, can be you. I must encourage you with 1 Thessalonians 2:19, 20. We take people with us into eternity. In verse 19, those you serve, will be your hope, joy, and crown of rejoicing, in the presence of Jesus, at His coming. Finally, in verse 20, **YOU ARE MY GLORY AND JOY.**

May these verses be yours in spiritual abundance (John 10:10).

I love you,
Paw Paw

On my 75th birthday, July 19, 2021, you guys surprised me with a big birthday weekend. It was more than amazing… except for me having Covid – I did not know it until Monday. But we all survived. At the party, you gave me this list of 75 things you love about me. Of course this list is a treasure AND it is accurate – LOL!
I love you my sweet family.

He has friends in lower places than Garth Brooks
That time he called me to see if I had any ideas for tutoring men in reading and writing via correspondence
Played invisible football with his big brother and loves to explain the rules
He has nicknames for everyone
He always has a project or something to teach us when he comes to visit
You never know who you are going to end up talking to when you call him on the phone
Been accepting collect phone calls from various prisons since the 70's

Road trips (even if he's driving) are FOR naps. And they're the best.
Consistently (and predictably) backs into parking spots
He always let Ron crank the heater in the Nova on the way home from karate. Year-round.
His custom-made duct tape and coke box car consoles
He travels with a year's worth of receipts and tax documents just in case he wants to make progress on... whatever it is he's doing with them
His commitment to signaling "Thanks!" in traffic by any means necessary
Takes sheer delight in knowing every mile marker south of the Mason Dixon line
WOW
WOWOWOWOWOWOWOW
WOWOWOWOWOWOWOW (with five!!!!!)
His liberal use of capitals and exclamations
Has mean grocery cart coasting skills
Hasn't found anything duct tape won't fix
Ends every text with "I LOVE YOU!!"
Motto: Don't run it under the driveway, just concrete over it!
DIY's with confidence
Got his green thumb on his bougainvilleas and showed them off with pride
ALWAYS has a challenge coin on hand
Has amazing card tricks... and magic tricks
And jokes
Somewhere, at some time, he attended his first rodeo
Refuses to die until Club Zion has fully repaid their debt to FBCCB
Has a staggering amount of faith in yellow Walmart rope
Has an amazing ability to turn any garage into a home office

And anywhere you can hook a hanger into a traveling closet
He gets his money's worth at a buffet (and then some)
Bacon!
Proud dumpster-diver for Macho products
Brown bowl + yellow blanket + footstool + Walker, Texas Ranger = a good night
Will not let paper maps (with hand-drawn illustrations) die in his lifetime
He came to meet every one of my babies within days of their births
Nothing is a "first rodeo" for him
"Hey, I'm easy to get along with!"
"Hey, I'm not such a bad guy!"
"Hey, stick with the kid!"
"Hey, I'm not just another pretty face!"
"We're making memories!"
"SAM THE RUNNING MAN!"
"Scootie GOOOOOOOOOOO Booty!"
"Has anyone ever told you how beautiful you are?"
"Yippie!"
"Cool beans!"
"POW!!"
"If you're waiting on me you're going backwards!"
"Have you seen my old house on Paul Jones Drive?"
"I LOVE road trips!"
"Do you have any hamburgers that are not older than five minutes?"
"Is it 'Kids Eat Free' night?"
He's the king of the Golden Corral
The only person I still get mail from (and I wouldn't have it any other way)
He always remembers important dates and anniversaries (and reminds me how loved we are by our special people)

Honored his parents in every action toward them
Welcomes the in-laws as if they are his own sons and daughters
Gives friendship freely and liberally
Seeks out the broken and downcast
Is committed to discipleship
Desires to train me to love God's Word and lead their families
Has a deep love for God's Word (and ragged Bibles to prove it)
He's humble
He sticks around for the long-haul
He's steady
Faithful
An encourager – one who gives courage to others
Intentional
Jovial
Selfless
A willing servant
The kind of Dad/Paw Paw who models the love of Christ to his children, his grands, and his great-grands

Happy 75th birthday to the very best Dad and Paw Paw any family could every ask for.

WE LOVE YOU!!!!!!!!!

MY EXTENDED GIFT TO YOU

The book is over, and I intentionally want these comments here. First, my heart's desire is for you to live for Jesus. Read 1 Corinthians 15:1-3; Romans 5:1-11; Romans 10:8-15; and 2 Corinthians 13:5. Make certain of your salvation. Next, the Bible tells us to study (2 Timothy 2:15). We are told to disciple (train) others: Matthew 28:18-20; John 15:16; 2 Timothy 2:2; Acts 11:26; and more. Over the years, I have written numerous Bible study booklets that will help you grow spiritually. I have written an entire, four year Bible College curriculum, and an extensive discipleship process for the next 80 years. Everything I have written is for you, and others like you. In 1 Thessalonians 2:19, 20, we take people with us into eternity. May our family be rich in Multi-Generational Faithfulness. Always remember: YOU are the first generation of your legacy.

I love you,
Paw Paw
Ephesians 3:20

> "Now unto Him that is able to do exceeding abundantly above all that we ask or think, according to the power that worketh in us..."
>
> — Ephesians 3:20

A letter written to me on January 6, 1966 from my Grandpappy

ATLANTA - THUR. JAN. 6 '66

MY SWEET NAMESAKE:

HOW GLAD I AM YOU ARE SWITCHING JOBS! I HAD HEARD THAT U. OF FLA. HAS 16,000 STUDENTS AND AN OVERLOADED FACULTY, SO-O-O COUNSELING BY PROFS IS NEGATIVE.

BUT YOU ARE ENTERING A NEW PERIOD OF SCHOOLING - WITH POSSIBILITIES AND POTENTIALITIES AND SEMBLANCE TO CAMPUS LIFE. APPROACH IT WITH AN ELEMENT OF JOY AND EAGERNESS. SOME TASKS MAY BE ROUGH AND TOUGH BUT THEY HAVE EDUCATIONAL VALUES - SEEK THEM, NOT THE DRUDGERIES. SERIOUS APPLICATION MAY BRING YOU A BID TO AN OFFICERS SCHOOL. YOU CAN CLAIM HIGH SCHOOL DIPLOMA, 1½ YEARS IN UNIVERSITY, TOP RANK IN DEMOLAY AND LITTLE LEAGUE B-B.! YOU HAVE <u>EVERYTHING</u> IN YOUR FAVOR: A GOOD NAME, - COAT OF ARMS MOTTO "FAITH IS EVERYTHING" DON'T LOSE SIGHT OF THAT; DON'T FAIL TO HOLD TO YOUR RELIGIOUS BELIEFS AND MORAL STANDARDS. WORK TO EXCEL & YOU'LL BE AN ADMIRAL.

DON'T BRUSH ASIDE QUICKLY A CAREER IN THE NAVY. BUT IF YOU DO, LET ME SUGGEST THAT YOU CONSIDER ONE OF THE NAVY'S SCHOOLS, ESPECIALY ELECTRONICS OR COMPUTER PROGRAMMERS AND YOU'LL DRIVE A CADILLAC AND YOUR WIFE WILL WEAR DIAMONDS.

WHEN YOU GET TO GR.L.NAV.TR. CENTER SEND US THE ENCLOSED ADDRESSED & STAMPED AIR MAIL CARD WITH ADDRESS - WE WON'T LET YOU DOWN.

Qué dios le bendiga (may God bless you)

Affectionately GRANDPAPPY.

Made in the USA
Columbia, SC
12 November 2023

26039753R00088